Ed

Enjoy Provide

a remarkable couple

all my best

2007

Words of Praise for *Driving the Career Highway*

"Career changes are a fact of life in today's world, and they will accelerate tomorrow. Knowing how best to compete is critical for people from 30 to 70. Reals Ellig and Morin give you the tools to make your next job yours . . . Read it cover to cover—then read it again."

—Jon A. Boscia, Chairman & CEO, Lincoln Financial Group

"I wish I had had the opportunity to read a book like *Driving the Career Highway* when I was starting my career. The 'warning signs' would have saved me hitting several 'bumps' in my career road. Very useful read!"

—Susan Whiting, CEO, Nielsen Media

"This book is unique in that it provides insightful and useful help for those faced with or considering mid-career change. Packed with pragmatic advice as well as tremendous tools to assist in doing a self-assessment and planning career changes. In this rapidly changing world with constantly changing organizations, almost everyone will at some time need to read this book."

—David A. Nadler, PhD Vice Chairman,
Marsh & McLennan Companies, Inc.

"As we manage to get through the traffic every day, it has become second nature to us to watch for signals and road signs. Why would that be any different as we are trying to manage our careers?"

—Ulrike Hildebrand, General Manager,
Human Resources, Mercedes-Benz USA

"Organizations have changed, and as a result so have careers. This is a valuable road map of the new career highways."

—Professor Edward E. Lawler, III, Marshall School of Business,
University of Southern California and Author of *Built to Change*

"Janice Reals Ellig and Bill Morin have done it *again*. For anyone whose career could use an overhaul—or even just a tune-up—*Driving the Career Highway* is a must-read. Loaded with fresh insights and practical, down-to-earth wisdom, it's an indispensable guidebook for navigating the murky terrain of corporate success today."

—*Fortune Magazine's* expert career columnist Ms. Anne Fisher ("Ask Annie"), Career columnist, *CNNmoney.com*

"The prospect of a job search change or a career change can be a frightening experience, especially for those in mid-career. Reals Ellig and Morin provide simple and straightforward tips for how to make career transitions more manageable and successful."

—Charles Tharp, Ph.D., Professor Human Resource Management, Rutgers University

"When career change occurs—especially when it's not of our choosing—even the smartest and most successful of us struggle with how to cope and survive. Reals Ellig and Morin offer professionals specific, practical ways to manage their careers through what are often very frightening periods."

—Johnny C. Taylor, Jr., J.D., SPHR Sr. Vice President, Human Resources, IAC/InterActiveCorp

"A practical guidebook for almost any point on the career highway. It's the next best thing to a personal coaching session with Bill or Janice. Share it with your coach/mentor and get ready to hit the accelerator !"

—Diane Gulyas, Group Vice President Dupont

"This is an inspirational and optimistic book because it gives the reader a clear road-map on how to self-manage a career."

—Mike Critelli, Chairman & CEO, Pitney Bowes

"Bill and Janice provide an indispensable map for reaching your career dream destination."

—Peter Thedinga, CLO, Bank of America

DRIVING THE CAREER HIGHWAY

20 ROAD SIGNS YOU CAN'T AFFORD TO MISS

JANICE REALS ELLIG

AND

WILLIAM J. MORIN

THOMAS NELSON
Since 1798

NASHVILLE   DALLAS   MEXICO CITY   RIO DE JANEIRO   BEIJING

BY JANICE:

*To my parents, Ann and Otto, who taught me the
value of having a career and loving the ride.
To my sister, Elaine, who supports me
with advice, love, and encouragement.
And to my husband, Bruce, a master at driving his career highway:
thank you for an adventurous and fun ride together . . .*

BY BILL:

*First, this book is dedicated to my coauthor,
Janice Reals Ellig, because she worked so diligently to finish
it in a first-class manner. I am grateful to her for her
outstanding commitment to our common endeavor.
I also want to dedicate this book to my wonderful
grandchildren, Knicole, Ivy, Jaiden, and Brianna.*

Published in Nashville, Tennessee, Thomas Nelson is a trademark of Thomas Nelson, Inc.

Thomas Nelson, Inc. titles may be purchased in bulk for educational, business, fund-raising, or sales promotional use. For information, please e-mail SpecialMarkets@ThomasNelson.com.

Library of Congress Cataloging-in-Publication Data

Ellig, Janice Reals.
    Driving the career highway : 20 road signs you can't afford to miss / Janice Reals Ellig and William J. Morin.
      p. cm.
    ISBN-13: 978-0-7852-2014-5 (hardcover)
    ISBN-10: 0-7852-2014-3
    1. Career development. I. Morin, William J. II. Title.
HF5381.E495 2007
650.1—dc22

                                       2006031081

Printed in the United States of America
07 08 09 10 QW 6 5 4 3 2 1

CONTENTS

FOREWORD

For the past ten years, I've had a peculiar job. As the *Fortune* magazine writer whose alter ego is CNNmoney.com's career-advice columnist ("Ask Annie"), I spend a good part of each day reading e-mails from people who hate their bosses. Or who fear that their bosses hate them. Or who are so bored in their jobs that they're ready to scream. Or who feel a vague sense that they're headed in the wrong direction, but can't pinpoint exactly how or why. Or who tried to change careers, failed, and are wondering, "Now what?" Or . . . (fill in your own career dilemma here).

Just about every possible work-related difficulty, setback, or quandary you can possibly imagine has crossed my desk at one time or another.

Here's a newsflash: The book you're about to read is a real-life guide to avoiding, forestalling, adjusting to, or curing all of those woes. And the authors, two of the smartest career advisers I know, do it with an admirable simplicity and in straightforward style.

Let's say, for instance, that you feel the urge to take stock of how your career is going so far—and what it may still be lacking. We all need to do this kind of assessment now and then. (As Will Rogers said, "Even if you're on the right track, you'll get run over if you just sit there.") The first three Road Signs in these pages will give you a clear picture of how you're doing, and how to make a big change if that's what's called for. Not getting along with your boss? Road Sign 8 is full of insights on learning to manage him or her, right from the start of a new job—or even before, by taking careful note of the boss's behavior in the interview—beginning with understanding who he or she really is and why. Want to figure out why you're not getting ahead in your company, despite your best efforts? The 10th Road Sign, "How to Compete So You Win," ought to be required reading for anyone puzzling over exactly what it takes to succeed in companies now.

And those are just a few of the essential topics Bill and Janice address with grace, wisdom, and good sense. I can't imagine any businessperson who couldn't glean some terrifically useful ideas from these pages, or find superb answers to any career-related question that might arise along the way.

In fact, if these two keep it up, they might just put me out of business.

ANNE FISHER
Senior Writer, *Fortune*
"Ask Annie," CNNmoney.com
Sullivan County, NY
August 2006

Your Career Highway: Where Is It Going? What Are the Road Conditions? How's Your Driving?

Enjoy the Ride—It's Your Life!

You're tooling along the career highway at 80 miles an hour.

The top is down on your new career car.

Your boss has spread sunshine on the roadway by telling you you're doing a "great job," and you're basking in the warmth of that approval under a bright blue sky.

All the other cars on the road are filled with supportive colleagues—and they're all going your way.

You see a sign some distance down the highway, but you can't quite make out what it says. Is it "Sharp Curves Ahead," or "Tunnel," or "Soft Shoulder"? You can't really tell, but you don't slow down in any event, because you have the breeze at your back, this baby drives like a dream, and there's nothing you can't handle with just a touch of the steering wheel.

Bang! Your company is sold. *Crash!* Your department is eliminated. *Whomp!* Your boss gets a big package and a new career car, and you are left on the side of the highway, standing next to the overturned wreck that was your career, watching the traffic speed past.

And the worst of it is, you never saw it coming.

CAREER MANAGEMENT
IN THE 21ST CENTURY

These days, there is simply no way professionals can have successful careers based solely on exceptional performance—without also proactively managing their own careers. In fact, managing your own career is as critical a task today as doing the job you were hired for. The reason? No one else is going to manage your career for you. Companies are too busy merging, acquiring, reverse acquiring, going bankrupt, and downsizing to pay attention to employees' career plans. Individual career development, once honored—at least in theory—by caring, forward-thinking organizations, is today defrauded by constantly changing expectations, sabotaged by other "priorities," or simply ignored.

The result is that even CEOs and those in the senior ranks find themselves ill equipped to manage their own careers effectively. The average lifespan of the CEO job today is three-plus years. Think about that: three years, about 1195 days, until a chief executive officer has moved on or been moved out. The polite term for it is "turnover"; the reality is more like a pileup of career car wrecks.

If CEOs and the top leadership are ill equipped to effectively manage their own careers, those of us farther down in the hierarchy are even worse off. No wonder corporate coach Kerry Sulkowics could assert in *Fast Company* magazine in February 2005 that "the unspoken truth of corporate life is that a lot of people in large organizations are unhappy, even miserable, at least every now and then . . . They feel lost, like small cogs in a much larger machine, or vulnerable and powerless."

Does the description fit you? Time to be the CEO in charge of your career.

WARNING! ROAD SIGN AHEAD

You don't have to be lost or miserable or vulnerable or powerless. If you don't know which way to go, it's probably because you're not reading the signs along the career highway. Yet no one in corporate America today can afford to miss these road signs. Miss a route marker, and you could be on your way to nowhere. Whiz by too fast to read the warning sign, and your car could end up in the career chop shop. Fail—or refuse—to notice the signs, and you could be heading for a career crash.

We've changed the names, but the following case studies are about real-life individuals—intelligent, ambitious, educated, the cream of corporate America, the best and the brightest—who really should have been able to read the signs and see what was coming . . .

Fresh out of business school, Doug Davis began work at XYZ Corporation, the renowned manufacturing giant that had long fueled the economy of the Midwest. Like his father before him, he went into training at XYZ's headquarters in one of the heartland's most bustling cities, and, also like his father, Doug expected to work his way up at the company, serve it loyally and well, and retire with a fat pension and a slim gold watch.

Twenty-two years later, American manufacturing barely existed, the bustling heartland city had become a ghost town, the Midwest's economy was on the skids, and Doug Davis was out of a job. Now he was not only wondering how he was going to make a living but was questioning his entire life—at forty-seven years old.

Paul Manning, thirty-two, was soaring up the corporate ladder on the back of his mentor, Warren Gordon, a star whose radiance lit up the entire big-bank galaxy. Paul had hitched his wagon tightly to the star. Universally known as "Gordon's guy," he bit the bullet and did Gordon's dirty work, knowing the payoff was to be at Gordon's side at each upward step.

Until one day: Warren Gordon had a fender bender with another highflier in the financial firmament—and came out on the short end of the deal.

"I'm really sorry, but this is the reality of corporate life," Warren said to Paul, as he slipped into his enormous golden parachute and wafted gently down to a long vacation, before being given the keys to another high-powered job. Manning had no parachute at all, nor was there a net available when he fell—hard—and found himself alone, at a dead standstill, and radioactive to anyone else in his organization—and his industry.

Carrie Edmonds had never needed a mentor. With a BA from Harvard, an MBA from Stanford, and enormous talent, she had always been on cruise control. Able to write her own ticket, she had written it in big, bold, colorful letters. There's nothing leisurely about the leisure industry, and Carrie had accelerated at supersonic speed from Day One. Her goal was to be an executive vice president by thirty-five; she made it when she was not quite thirty-four.

She now strode through her company like the heir apparent she so clearly was, the unquestioned star of her industry. She had what she'd always wanted—her foot on the gas pedal of a powerful engine, and her hands on the steering wheel of almost limitless resources to execute her long-cherished vision for the sizable empire that was now her responsibility.

And suddenly, it wasn't enough. The fulfillment she had planned to gain by her success simply wasn't there. The woman who used to charge out of bed so she could get to work early found herself lying under the covers in the morning, listening to the clock ticking and trying to decide if she had the guts to skip her first meeting.

THE DRIVING HAZARD

What happened to these three? How did they end up crashing and burning—out, down, and disappointed—when it seemed they had everything going for them and everything to look forward to?

There is a simple answer to these questions but a complex reality behind it. The simple answer is that, in addition to their talent, intelligence, and education, the three possessed the same very pat assumptions and expectations as most people in corporate life. Acting on these, they drove ahead blindly into a complex reality, where they missed the road signs along the career highway—the danger signals that would have alerted them to potholes, detours, curves in the road, and the dangers or opportunities that just might be lurking around one of those curves. When you miss warning signs, you're bound to suffer the consequences.

We've seen this time after time, but never more so than in today's economic reality, so unlike the reality today's corporate professionals expected, planned for, trained for, and worked for. Individuals who perform brilliantly at managing the financials or devising and executing the strategic plan all too often fall apart when it comes to managing their own careers. In our view, based on decades of experience in human resources and executive coaching, they fail the career self-management task because they simply don't see those clear warning signs, the noisily blinking directional signals, the compass indicators going haywire—until it's too late.

Even more fundamentally, they fail to understand that there *are* such signs along the career highway. Had Doug, Paul, and Carrie been aware of the signs, and had they read them right, it might have prompted some questions: What's wrong? Is it me? The job? The organization? The people I work with? If only these three, and thousands of others, had pulled off the corporate highway to assess their surroundings—to ask questions, find answers, and maybe even change direction—their jobs today might still be on track—careers that would be not just a good living, but a good life.

The complex reality behind the simple answer to career crashes is that, while today's career is not a straight, certain, direct way up, there *are* signs along the route that show the way—if you're not blind to them. Unfortunately, such blindness is deadly in a world in which the old rules no longer apply.

The old rules were about working hard and being rewarded for it, about finding your niche and filling it forever. The old rules said that the greater the power and perks, the greater the self-fulfillment. The old rules assured you that Mother Corporation and her assiduous HR department were there to hand you a career road map the day you walked in the door that would guide you to your retirement party forty years later. Remember those extensive career ladder charts HR produced? Where are they now?

Gone—along with the old rules, which, by the way, have not been replaced by new rules. It is unlikely that they will be. There are no more career road maps to hand out. Today's organizations' men and women—even the best and the brightest—are driving alone.

ROADSIDE ASSISTANCE NEEDED

Lacking the guidance of old, the ranks of corporate America are today filled with people who are burned-out, worn-out, or washed-out—on the brink of failure, a nervous breakdown, despair, or all three. Above all, they're confused. Their assumptions about their career pathways have proven to be unfounded. The reality of their work life and of their life's work simply isn't meeting their expectations.

They're driving a highway that is unfamiliar to them, that lacks recognizable landmarks, that's taking them they-don't-know-where. They feel as if they are stuck in a high-speed traffic circle in the middle of a multihighway cloverleaf, going around and around aimlessly. Worst of all, they can't find the brake or the accelerator, and now the steering has gone out of control. They need emergency roadside assistance: a car that works, a map, a compass, and a companion guidebook to let them know what they're seeing along the route.

That's precisely what you'll find in this book.

Simply put, we'll tell you how to read the signs so you can keep your career on the right road and moving at the right speed toward the right destination.

It's an essential guide, for in today's world driving the career highway is a solo journey. Chances are you paid a lot for the car you're driving. You've invested heavily in this trip. There's a place you want to get to up ahead—and of course, you also want to enjoy the ride. To do that, you need to be prepared to deal with the bumps, cracks, and obstacles along the highway.

We know the highway well. For one thing, we've both been part of corporate life—as managers and entrepreneurs—for decades. We've seen our own signs on our own career highways. We also admit we missed a few—and lived to regret it.

Mostly, however, in our combined sixty years of coaching and executive recruiting, we've seen what happens when individuals fail to read the signs along the career highway . . . or ignore the signs . . . or decide the signs couldn't possibly apply to them . . . or simply refuse to pay attention.

We're here to remind you to pay attention.

From all those years of working with folks who failed to see the signs—or to read them right—we've distilled the twenty most compelling problems/situations/instances that can cause you to detour, stall, get lost, or crash and burn on your career highway.

Maybe you're dissatisfied with your job; worried about downsizing, upgrading, or outsourcing; uncertain where you stand with the boss; unclear about your colleagues' intentions. It could be you're unhappy with the route you're on, feel you're being passed by too many others, or are worried about losing control of your career vehicle. All of these are road signs we'll help you read and interpret. More than that, we'll assign you tasks that will prepare you to deal with what the signs are warning you about *beforehand*—so that you don't lose control, don't get passed by others, and do drive on a highway that is as fulfilling and rewarding as you hoped when you first got in the car and turned the key in the ignition.

It's your career. Get ready to drive it safely, smoothly, and successfully to the destination you've dreamed about.

Ladies and Gentlemen, start your engines . . . Ready to be the CEO in charge of your career?

Who Are You? Where Have You Been? Where Do You Really Want to Go?

Bill: In recruiting candidates for searches, do you find people in corporate America generally happy or unhappy in their careers?

Janice: For too many, it's a matter of habit, not happiness.

Bill: And too many have accepted that happiness in a career is simply not possible.

Janice: Yes. That's why I advise just about every candidate who comes through my office to stop and evaluate who they are, to take a look in the rearview mirror to see where they've been, and only then to figure out where they want to go. The job I am interviewing them for may fit their experiences, but may not be right for what they really want to do next. For the most part, they have not stopped to evaluate other possibilities; they just continue driving on a career highway—it becomes what they *know* best, not what *is* best!

Bill: There are times when you just need to take a break, turn on the lights, and look objectively at every aspect of your life. We just need to stop and reassess.

Janice: Otherwise, you run the risk of crashing and burning. But people are simply afraid that if they stop, they won't be able to start again.

Bill: Actually, they'll get off the mark faster, smoother, and better if they take that all-important pause.

FAILURE TO STOP CAN BE DANGEROUS

Remember the rules about what to do at a Stop sign? You're required to bring your vehicle to a complete stop, check your rearview mirror, look carefully to the right and left, and, of course, scan the road ahead. Only when you are completely satisfied that the conditions are right and that your way is clear can you take your foot off the brake and put it back on the accelerator.

Chances are that you're reading this book because you feel you're driving toward some sort of intersection in your career. Maybe you see a Stop sign ahead. Maybe you're there, with your foot on the brake and the engine idling, waiting for the other cars to get out of the way. And maybe you're not quite sure what that sign up there is saying, and you figure you don't need to slow up; you'll just ram through.

Don't.

Failure to stop at a Stop sign is as dangerous in a career as it is on the road. The message it's giving you is all-important: if you don't stop, look, listen, and assess right now, your career may not make it out of the intersection at all.

So hit the brakes.

Not tomorrow. Today. Now. This minute.

Put down the BlackBerry. Close the cell phone. Clear your mind. It's time for a pause.

STOP—BUT DON'T NECESSARILY STOP WORKING: THE PAUSE THAT REFRESHES

High school kids sometimes take a "gap year" before they start classes at their prospective colleges. Partly it's because they are utterly exhausted—burned-out—from all the pressure to get into college. And partly it's a way of promoting "discovery of one's own passions," as an admissions officer at Harvard put it—Harvard being just one of many fine institutions of higher learning that actually advises students to experience the gap year before college.

Professors often take sabbaticals after seven years of steady teaching and scholarship. The mind begins to tire if it concentrates too consistently on any one thing. A change of both pace and scenery refreshes the brain's capabilities and restores its capacity for thinking.

Even television sitcoms and dramas go on hiatus so the writers, directors, actors, designers, etc., can rest and reinvigorate their creativity. After all, how many plots are there in the world—and how many jokes can you make about dysfunctional families?

In all of these cases, the value of the pause that refreshes has been recognized. Now it's time to recognize its value in a career.

Think about it. On any long road trip, you must put on the brakes now and again. You need to take the time to reassess, now that you've been on the road for a while, whether you want the fastest route, the scenic highway, or the route that meanders through all those towns and cities. You need time to take the car in for some maintenance—to make sure that the engine is sound, that the air bags will still work if needed, that your tire treads are good enough to take you through bad weather and over rough roads. You need time to adjust the rearview mirror, to make sure you can see with absolute clarity where you've been and what's coming up behind you. And you need time to rethink your destination, to make absolutely sure you know where it is you want to go.

To do all that, you simply have to stop.

But let's be clear: we are not advising that you necessarily stop working. We're in no way hinting that you should quit your job, although a vacation or leave isn't a bad idea, as we'll suggest a bit later. Nor are we talking about blank downtime—an empty stretch of doing and thinking nothing. After all, high school kids spend their gap year doing something "else"—maybe traveling to exotic places or signing on to some form of community service—something that enriches their education. Professors on sabbatical take the opportunity to work on a subject important to them. And TV actors make a movie or do dinner theater or head for Broadway. Stopping, therefore, isn't for vegetating; it's for stretching. It isn't doing nothing that refreshes you; it's doing something different, something for *you*.

What we have in mind is doing something for you by stretching your mind, your life, yourself— taking time for assessment and evaluation of you, your goals, where you're coming from, where you want to get to, and whether you can and should go there. And for that, you'll have to stop your forward motion for a bit.

Why is this so important? Because we've seen too many bright,

> We spend most of our time and energy in a kind of horizontal thinking. We move along the surface of things . . . [but] there are times when we stop. We sit still. We lose ourselves in a pile of leaves or its memory. We listen and breezes from a whole other world begin to whisper.
>
> —JAMES CARROLL, COLUMNIST

talented, ambitious individuals crash and burn—only to discover, as they picked themselves up out of the wreckage, that they crashed and burned for something they didn't really care about. Had they seen the Stop sign staring them in the face and come to the required complete halt, they might have heard that all-important inner voice telling them what it is they really love, what it is that holds meaning for them, what would give their lives purpose so that they wouldn't crash and burn at all.

But to hear that inner voice, you have to listen. And for that, you must stop your headlong rush. You must pause. And you must establish the conditions for hearing what the inner voice is telling you.

That's what the first road sign on the career highway is all about. In a very real sense, if you don't get this one right, the others won't matter very much. Let's face it: without the passion for a purpose, no career is really worth it.

So follow this road sign's instruction: bring yourself to a complete stop, and get ready to look back, gaze forward, and do some important maintenance. In doing so, you'll take your thinking beyond what you are doing to find not just what you know, but what you know is right for you.

OUR STOP SIGNS

Some personal history first.

The truth is that both of us have met Stop signs in our careers, and we both agree that the pauses that followed were invaluable. The irony in our cases—and it will doubtless turn out the same for you—is that the stops were the reason that our careers really got moving in the right direction and on faster, smoother tracks.

Bill hit his first Stop sign early in his chosen career as a schoolteacher. He has always loved teaching. To this day, he can't think of a higher honor in life than being asked a question. So as a young man, he went out and got two MS degrees to prepare himself for this noble profession. But in time, the rising financial pressures of a growing family proved too burdensome. Bill drove right up to the Stop sign and came to a complete halt so he could rethink, determine how he could better accomplish his goals, find a balance between personal needs and his family's economic needs, and see where he could fit. The Stop taught him two things. One, he decided to change direction and head toward corporate America in order to do better economically. Two, he listened to that inner voice telling him that he had to in some way keep the essence of teaching in his life.

Bill hit his second Stop sign in quite a different way, and the pause this time was of a different nature: it helped him draw a line he would not cross. As a product manager in a major food company, he was assigned to carry out an exhaustive study of a proposed new product, still in development. He did so, then reported—accurately—that the product was subpar and not likely to succeed. For reasons that can only be guessed at, Bill's supervisor didn't want to hear that. He called Bill a "dope" for knocking the product, and he ordered him to water down the report.

Of course, Bill refused. But the incident forced him to halt, look around, and reevaluate whether he fit in this organization. He decided he did not, that his style conflicted too much with the company's political emphasis. His inner voice told him that both the industry he was in and the style of the organization went against his grain, so Bill changed both.

The result of these stops for Bill? He found a home in business, but in situations where he could create a one-on-one classroom. Over time, he kept "refining" the situation. Today, he manages his own executive coaching firm. He is still a scholar who consistently studies and observes. He constantly keeps abreast of the latest research. And he is able to bring all that to bear in a setting in which people still ask him questions.

For Janice, the first Stop sign came in the form of a corporate reorganization that changed some of what she wanted to do and challenged most of the career assumptions on which she had been operating. After twenty years in corporate America, she realized for the first time that she did not feel in control of her own professional destiny. At about the same time, she got together with a guy she had known professionally for fifteen years—the head of Drake, Beam Morin, Inc., international consultants—namely, Bill Morin. She and Bill decided they had a book to write, and they began work on their jointly authored *What Every Successful Woman Knows: 12 Breakthrough Strategies to Get the Power & Ignite Your Career.* The two incidents—the unanticipated reorganization that stymied her career progression, and embarking on a journey toward a whole new kind of work—forced her to rethink where she had been and where she was going. She realized that the direction she'd been following was not taking her where she wanted to be down the road. Rather, this new direction—interviewing and speaking directly to other women in corporate America through writing and lecturing—was much more in tune with the leanings of her inner voice.

While writing the book over a two-year period, and while still fully engaged in her corporate role, she reassessed her options and thought hard about what her next career step might be: she talked to people, read books, and evaluated her passion for a change. Several career options presented themselves, but they seemed neither here nor there, until she came upon the one that seemed to fit her personality and skill set: executive search.

Janice's second Stop sign came as a real shock to her. Enticed into the executive search industry by a large and prestigious firm, she soon realized that the firm's size and prestige, while certainly real, obscured the way things actually worked at the firm. A mere three weeks into the role, Janice's inner voice told her clearly that this particular company was not for her. She was truly surprised by this experience, but she was also quick to act and move on.

Brief as the experience had been—and as mismatched with the place as she had felt—even this abbreviated encounter was enough to convince Janice that executive search was the career she wanted to pursue; it clearly resonated powerfully with the direction she was charting. She immediately moved to a highly respected boutique search firm as a full partner in charge of originating and executing her searches—in a way that was more in line with her values and her ideas about how to conduct searches. There she was, fully in control of her business and able to use her twenty years of human resources experience in corporate America to be a true search *consultant*— one who knew the environment and understood corporate dynamics. Today, she is co-owner and Co-CEO of that company. She is also well positioned to speak with authority to and about women in corporate America, and she continues to write books.

> Never continue in a job you don't enjoy. If you're happy in what you're doing, you'll like yourself, you'll have inner peace. And if you have that, along with physical health, you will have had more success than you could possibly have imagined.
>
> —Johnny Carson
> 1925–2005

Obviously, these narratives are totally individual. Your Stop sign might look entirely different; your inner voice is unique. But we tell you about these personal experiences because we both believe that had we not paid attention to the Stop signs on our career highways, our careers and our lives would not have been as fulfilling, as purposeful, as happy as they have been. Before you crash, before you get to a certain point in your life only to realize you've missed the boat, take the pause that refreshes: reassess and reevaluate your career and what you want from it. Do it and, like both of us, you'll resume normal speed for your next career move. In fact, you'll go faster.

DAY BY DAY

Such a reassessment/reevaluation takes time, and it should not be rushed. Look at Janice's case: it was a two-year process to consider a career change. Her life didn't stop. Neither did her work. She still had a significant role in corporate America at the time; she was busy writing a book with Bill; she was serving on the boards of directors of a number of not-for-profit organizations. She was as busy and energetic as ever. But she stopped to evaluate her life, her goals, and the direction in which she was going, and she took the time to investigate other directions and explore other options.

Janice used the time to speak to a great many people in the search business—people she herself had hired when she was a human resources director in charge of selecting search firms. She attended search association conferences. She talked to trusted friends and advisors—the most important and valuable being her husband, an accomplished HR professional. All this and a lot of self-evaluation through reading and self-testing occupied her during those twenty-four months—one day at a time.

EACH DAY IS A LIFE

You live your life one day at a time. Every morning when you wake up, it's equivalent to a rebirth. And when you go to sleep at the end of the day, that is akin to a death. That means that every day is a fresh chance; it also means that you dare not let the days pass you by. So the best way to begin this important time of assessment and reevaluation is by gathering all the data you can on your life, and the best way to do that is by taking a look at how you live day by day.

TASK 1: START A DAILY JOURNAL

Personal journaling is as effective a method as there is for examining your life. The very process of writing—thinking what you're going to say, organizing it, finding the right way to express it—requires reflection about the subject, as well as effort and patience. When the subject is you—your achievements, your disappointments, your thoughts—the process forces you to not just observe but to actually analyze your life and your career. We recommend two rules for the journaling task.

Do it every day. Make journaling as automatic a habit as brushing your teeth. Your daily entry need not be long. It need not be written in elegant, carefully composed sentences, and it doesn't have to express your innermost thoughts—although it may, if you wish. Write it in the shortest shorthand you like. Use abbreviations. Express yourself in secret code if you want to. The important thing is just to get something down; what counts is not the prose but the persistence.

> In the name of God,
> stop a moment,
> cease your work,
> look around you.
> —LEO TOLSTOY,
> RUSSIAN WRITER,
> 1828–1910

Our personal preference—and our suggestion—is that you do a diary entry as soon as you wake up. In *The Artist's Way: A Spiritual Path to Higher Creativity*, author Julia Cameron recommends that you let the words you write in your journal be a free flowing of thoughts. In other words, don't really think about what you want to say; just let the thoughts spill out. (As you'll see in a bit, we highly recommend this book.)

Review your journal once a month. Again, make it automatic. Set up a recurring appointment on your calendar for "journal review," on the fifteenth of every month, on the second Thursday, or whatever day you're comfortable with. Just make sure you keep the appointment once a month. This is your *rearview mirror*, and if you don't check it out carefully, you could easily find your career—and your life—rammed from the rear.

Note the pluses and minuses, the high points and the disasters of the last thirty days. Think about all this: What caused or preceded or in some way influenced both the former and the latter? Above all, look each month to see if there has been an upward tick. Have you learned anything new? Have you advanced—not just up the career ladder but in terms of enriching your life and/or bringing yourself closer to goals of fulfillment and happiness? Where does your review show you going? Is there a pattern, a trend of negatives or positives? If so, what is it telling you about what is going right or wrong, badly or well, and what can you do to turn the negative into a positive? After all, life is a journey; that's why keeping track of it is so valuable—and that's why they call it a journal.

But while only you can do this kind of self-inspection/introspection, that doesn't mean you shouldn't reach out for help from others. Asking for directions or help along your career highway makes sense; everyone needs some assistance from time to time, and we encourage everyone: when you need help, ask for it.

GET A DIFFERENT PERSPECTIVE: EXPAND YOUR HORIZONS

Have you ever listened to your recorded voice? It doesn't sound like your voice at all. It's not the voice you hear when you're speaking to others. It can't be. You're the only one in the world who hears your voice your way—through ears pinned behind the voice. Everyone else, after all, hears your voice coming at them directly.

In the same way, you can't always see your life head-on as others do, so it's often helpful to find out just what others see when they look at your life. Indeed, under any circumstances, but especially if your monthly review has come up with more negatives than positives, it is valuable to discuss your looming career intersection with someone you trust.

TASK 2: FIND A COACH, COUNSELOR, OR FRIEND, AND TALK IT THROUGH

Though you trust your close friends and family members, they can be the least effective of "counselors" when it comes to helping you think about your career. The reason is simple: because your friends and family members love you, they want you to be happy. Their tendency is to comfort you, to tell you that "things will work out all right" or that "you'll get over it." Although soothing, such advice is not particularly helpful.

So think about consulting a professional. After all, you go to a professional physician when your health is at issue and to a professional accountant or financial planner for help in thinking through the state of your finances. Shouldn't you consider seeing a professional counselor when assessing and evaluating whether your career is taking you where you want to go?

There is a wide range of skill sets and job titles that fit the description of "professional counselor." There are executive coaches, like Bill, who routinely counsel people on their career goals and how to strategize to achieve them. There are career psychologists. There are trained social workers, who specialize in helping professionals navigate among resources. Your college alumni office may even have a referral service for these kinds of services.

But in addition to the career experts, there are also the life experts. Your pastor or priest; a trusted older professional, especially someone who has had a similar career and may have survived similar doubts or concerns; a favorite mentor, maybe a family friend or former teacher or athletic coach—may be the perfect person to turn to.

In essence, you're looking for someone who can bring order out of chaos, who won't shoot from the hip but will reflect with you and help you sort through the confusion in a framework of safety. Most of all, the individual needs to be one who will provide a balanced, utterly unprejudiced and unprejudged perspective. It must be someone you trust, who has your best interest at heart in an unbiased way, and who will be there to provide nonjudgmental feedback. This chart may help you think about who that person might be:

TALK IT OUT—ASK FOR DIRECTIONS

Seek Out Others	Their Advice/Perspective
Friends	
Family	
Internal Mentors	
Professional Colleagues/ Peers in Other Organizations	
Coaches	

Community Leaders/ Not-for-Profit Colleagues	
Religious Affiliates	
Others	

The aim of such counseling? Action! An answer to the question, what do I do next? What you need from others is that all-important gentle nudge forward—the one that will get your vehicle pointed in the right direction, start your motor again, and send you heading through the intersection when the time is right.

DRIVING DIRECTIONS

At this point, you may not even know exactly where you're going. Still, you ought to be thinking about heading toward a general compass direction, and you should have some idea which road you want to drive on.

TASK 3: EDUCATE YOURSELF—CONSTANTLY

You're not the first or only person to have hit a career Stop sign. And we're not the first or only people to have written a book suggesting ways to get through the intersection and back on the highway. There are literally tens of thousands of books out there, representing a vast range of expert advice and varied responses. Take advantage of this huge body of work, and figuratively pick the brains of the many disparate people offering suggestions. Suggestions about ways to think about your future, about fresh possibilities for fulfillment, about pathways to purpose you may never have considered before. The subject is vast, and so are the possible responses.

We have our favorites—from the highly spiritual *The Artist's Way* by Julia Cameron, to the straightforward interpersonal advice of *The Office Survival Guide* by Marilyn Puder-York, to Jack Welch's hard-hitting *Winning* and, an obvious favorite for us both, Bill Morin's *Total Career Fitness: A Complete Checkup and Workout Guide.* But our favorites may not strike a chord with you, so browse your neighborhood's bookstores and libraries—and by all means search the Internet—for voices that resonate with you. Let what you achieved in Tasks 1 and 2 guide and focus your search. In carrying out those tasks, you talked to yourself and to others about what's lacking in your career and how you might get yourself and your professional life back on the road. Both sets of conversations should have churned up keywords that can direct your browsing.

And don't stop there. Attend lectures, sign up for seminars, take a class, or even go on retreat to sample the possibilities. The voice that speaks directly to you is surely out there; you have a better chance of hearing it if you put your ear to the ground.

EXTERNAL EVENTS/EXPERIENCES

Books to Read/Skim	What I Learned
Conferences to Attend	What I Learned
Classes to Attend	What I Learned
Retreats	What I Learned

Professionals/Speakers I Want to Hear	What I Learned
Other External Factors	What I Learned

This is really all about education, and it doesn't stop when you've heard the voice and addressed the issue. In this, as in every other aspect of life, education should be ongoing. Even those of us who are happy and personally fulfilled in their professional lives should "keep up" with the new thinking about all this as we both try to every day. After all, we never know what might speed up our drive along the career highway—or make it safer or more enriching.

GET READY FOR THE RIDE

Two tasks remain before you can safely make it through the intersection. Both prepare you for the ride ahead.

TASK 4: DROP THAT HEAVY BAGGAGE

Later on in this book, you'll be asked to think about what you might like to be in life if there were no restrictions at all on your dreams or even your fantasies. Task 4 is good preparation for that, because, of course, there are restrictions in our lives, and here is where you'll take a good look at yours—and put them aside.

We grow up with all sorts of restrictions—a range of shoulds, can'ts, don'ts, and more: Don't wrinkle your party dress! No ball playing in the house! Turn down that music! Stop running in the hallways!

The social environment imposes a lot more, laying down "rules" about appearance, public behavior, acceptable values, and such social norms as sex and drinking. Beyond those restrictions, just about everything we do and everyone we know affects or at least influences what we come to see as the boundaries of our lives. An older sibling, our religion, the schools we attend—all may prescribe and define our lives and our behavior.

As we go through life, these prescriptions and definitions harden into fears or prohibitions that can impede us in ways great or small. Here's a seemingly small example, yet it inhibited Janice for years from doing something she truly wanted to do—namely, speak French fluently. She thinks the fear originated back in high school French class when she was reciting out loud and someone in the class giggled. Her embarrassment intensified the reluctance most of us feel in trying to speak a foreign language, and for years when Janice traveled abroad, she did not dare say anything in French beyond ordering a meal—afraid that her pronunciation wouldn't be good enough, that she would make a mistake, or that people would laugh. It was a bit of baggage she didn't even realize she was still carrying.

One summer, while traveling in Provence, she met a group of people from Ohio. They were speaking French with heavy American accents and an occasional grammatical error, but with no fear whatsoever. No one was giggling; no one was laughing at them. In fact, the French seemed pleased at the group's attempts to speak their language.

Janice immediately unfroze, opened her mouth, and out came French. She dropped her heavy baggage on a beach along the Côte d'Azur and never picked it up again.

Janice's fear of speaking French was the kind of baggage that can truly limit our imaginations and hold us back from doing what we really want to do in life. And this is especially the case because such limits are almost always self-imposed. So what if some kid in high school giggled? What did that have to do with the French language? So what if your older brother laid down the law? You certainly didn't have to believe every word he said. As for religion, you could have—should have—questioned what was handed down to you; it's the best way to shore up your faith. And as for being a product of your school, you're out of school now, and you're on your own.

You say your parents are to blame? You know what? No one is really well schooled in parenting. Every parent on earth goes through on-the-job training, and all have made mistakes. Your parents were definitely imperfect—and so are the children they produced! It's time to stop blaming Mom and Dad. After all, they gave you life. Now it is up to you to live it without continuing to blame them, or anyone else, for the baggage you're carrying. It is history—learn from it so you don't repeat mistakes, but stop wallowing in the might-have-beens, could-have-beens, and should-have-beens. It's time to stop being held back by these restrictions; it's time to put down the baggage.

This task asks you to identify the things that are telling you what you cannot do. It is a very private exercise, but you may well want to consult a trusted friend to help you through it, because sometimes others can see the baggage we're carrying better than we ourselves can.

First, we're going to suggest some of the most common pieces of baggage you might be carrying—you can certainly add others—and we're going to ask you to think about how each of these may be holding you back from fulfilling yourself in a way that is true to you.

Potential Piece of Baggage in Your Life	What View of Yourself Does This Piece of Baggage Leave You With?	What Does It Make You Afraid Of?	How Is This Holding You Back?
Family Background			
Family Dynamics			
Religion			
Schooling			
Friends			
An Event in the Past			
A Personality Trait			
A Physical Characteristic			
A Mental Issue			
Other			

Now that you've identified what may be holding you back, it's time to free yourself. Using your analysis from above, label each suitcase below appropriately. Name the baggage—My Upbringing, My Religion, etc.—and assess whether it is weighing you down because you're continuing to carry it.

🧳 My Baggage _____

🧳 My Baggage _____

Throw away the luggage. X out the pictures or write yourself a luggage tag that sends each piece of baggage to a deserted island a million miles away. Either way, set all your bags down. You have the strength to do so. After all, you were the one who picked them up in the first place.

SERVICE AREA AHEAD: FOOD AND FUEL

Right now, replenish yourself before getting back on the highway. Reflect. Test out what you've learned. Every highway has its service areas, where drivers can pull in, walk the dog, wash up, kick back a bit, and refuel both their cars and themselves before taking up the journey again. Take time for a service stop now.

TASK 5: TAKE A SABBATICAL WITH YOURSELF—DO AN ENGINE CHECK

Remember that inner voice we talked about earlier? Sometimes it's hard to hear when you're around others. So take some time by yourself, and think about what you've gained and what you've cast off in completing the tasks in this chapter.

But don't just take a vacation. A solitary walk on the beach will reveal only that the ocean is huge and the number of grains of sand immense. Those are accurate revelations, but they won't get you very far. The point of taking a sabbatical with yourself is to create a plan.

Keep in mind the original meaning of the word *sabbatical*: the idea was that every seventh year, farmland would be left fallow—plowed but unseeded—so that the following year, it would be even more fertile. The fallow year offered the soil an opportunity to replenish its nutritional content so that the next harvest would be better than ever.

From your service-area sabbatical, you want to harvest a view of your future that may not be forever but that certainly offers the potential for new opportunities. So spend whatever time it takes—alone—to do the assessing and evaluating that will open your brain to such opportunities.

The plan doesn't need to be comprehensive. But it should have a defined goal for your fulfillment and a general idea of how to get there. Above all, it should add clarity to your life and purpose to your career. If it doesn't, start over and do this chapter's tasks again till you get it right. Here's a primer of basic sabbatical tasks:

MY SABBATICAL TASKS

Tasks	What Is This Task Telling Me?
Review My Journal Monthly	
Identify My Trusted Advisors	
Choose Some Books to Read This Year, and List Them	

Select Two Conferences to Attend in the Next Three Months	
Identify My Two New External Experiences	
Identify the Dropped Baggage	

Now, get back in your car, check all the dashboard lights, glance again in your rearview mirror, and scan the road ahead. All clear? Drive on. Head to your destination, but keep an eye out for that next road sign up ahead . . .

SUMMARY

Like life, every career needs a reassessment now and again. The fact that you're reading this book means the moment is right for you to reassess, rethink, reevaluate. Here's how to go about this important process:

1. Start a daily journal.
2. Find a coach, counselor, or friend, and talk it through.
3. Educate yourself—constantly.
4. Drop your baggage.
5. Take a sabbatical—do an engine check.

> Take rest; a field that has rested gives a bountiful crop.
>
> —OVID, ROMAN POET, 43 BC–17 AD

Live Your Dream:
Make a Career Change

Janice: Do you find that people often feel trapped by careers that have simply stopped working for them? They can't seem to find a way out?

Bill: I've noticed this more and more since 9/11, and I see it a lot in my coaching practice. The predicament reminds me of that aerial view of the circle around the Arch of Triumph in Paris, with all the cars whizzing around it. The cars on the inside —the people who are trapped in a career they don't want— just have no way to get over to an exit. They can't even see the exit.

Janice: It breeds frustration and a lot of anger, although I think the underlying emotion is fear.

Bill: Right. They hang on instead. Then the frustration level goes even higher, and they blame the job, the company, others.

Janice: Or they panic and get off wherever they can—and it's the wrong road altogether. Changing careers is risky, and people are naturally risk-averse. As someone once said, "Only babies like a change."

YOU'VE CHANGED:
EXPLORE THE CHOICES

Eager and optimistic at age twenty-something, you set off excitedly on the career of your choice.

Twenty years later—sometimes even ten—that same career has gone stale, and you wonder how you could ever have thought that this choice was right for you.

What happened? How has the career you yearned for, trained for, and invested in so heavily now become a perpetual-motion treadmill that you can't get off of—one that has you going in circles, with no exit in sight?

There's an easy answer to that: you've changed. At forty, the person you were at twenty can look like a total stranger. The things that stranger cared about, the things he or she wanted from a career, may be utterly unrecognizable. And that is good, of course. That is what living is all about. In that time of living, you experienced a little bit of the good, the bad, and the ugly—and you came to know yourself better. And with each new person, experience, and event you learned from in life, you should also have seen that there are more choices out there than you ever imagined.

> So many of our dreams at first seem impossible, then they seem improbable, and then, when we summon the will, they soon become inevitable.
>
> —CHRISTOPHER REEVE, ACTOR, 1952–2004

Careers can change too. They evolve in their own ways, and not all of the developments are subject to your control. When you change in one direction and/or your career changes in another, you end up on the treadmill—in constant motion, but not getting anywhere.

But in a career, as in life, change also brings more options, so be ready to explore them with your eyes wide open.

FIND THE RIGHT OFF-RAMP

But first you need to start thinking about finding the off-ramp—about getting out of this career and into something else.

Of course, it may well be the case that career change is not your idea. Maybe you're being downsized. Maybe you've been summarily fired. Perhaps it's become clear that your skills are simply no longer (a) needed, (b) up to snuff, or (c) relevant. Maybe your field has changed so radically that the career you once knew has just vanished—gone the way of the blacksmith or the keypunch operator.

However you got here—whether on your own or driven by circumstances—you're in a bad place: going around in circles but never going forward, searching frantically across a wall of traffic for a way out, wondering how you can ever position yourself to exit. In the words of the old song about "That Old Black Magic," made famous by Frank Sinatra, you're "in a spin," so "down and down you go, round and round you go." And as you keep searching for an exit, cars outside the circle are lining up, ready to pounce into the circle and cut you off each time you make for the off-ramp. No wonder you're in a panic.

> There is no security on this earth, there is only opportunity.
>
> —GENERAL DOUGLAS MACARTHUR, 1880–1964

It's a dilemma that takes considerable effort to resolve, and the effort is twofold. First, you must extricate yourself from the career that is no longer working, and second, you must launch yourself into something new. Starting over is never easy, of course, and it can be particularly arduous at the midpoint of a career, or following a downsizing or a termination that feels like failure, or if it is accompanied by a sense of loss or disillusionment.

But by making *career change* your job—your business, your key objective—the dilemma can be resolved, and you can stop spinning aimlessly. To do so successfully, you must bring to the task the same care and deliberation you brought to launching your first career—only now you have experience and maturity to add to the mix. To end your old career, you will need the same forward-looking perspective you had in your twenties; to embark on something new, you'll need the same willingness to learn and a similar sense of adventure. Plan it right, take it step-by-step, and you can make a midcourse correction that will be not just a career change but a life renewal as well.

Back at the Stop sign, you had to take time to assess where you've been and where you are currently going. Here, you are looking at an Exit to get you on your next career road—the right road. This chapter offers you a seven-task process for doing so. You'll find it a little like taking your first step as a toddler. Ironically, back then you had little fear of falling even though you faced the biggest learning curve of your life. You can feel that way again now if you follow the process in this chapter.

THE MADONNA FACTOR

The evidence is fairly clear that everyone is going to need such a process in due course. Current projections are that those entering the workforce today will change careers as frequently as the preceding generation changed jobs. That works out to some half a dozen career changes in a lifetime—maybe more.

Call it the "Madonna factor." The Material Girl went from pop idol to movie star to mother, wife, and author in the space of two decades—and who can say what's next for her? Her role changes have been near reincarnations, as she seems to have evolved from a blue-collar know-nothing to a quasi aristocrat with just a touch of an upper-class British accent.

Of course, there's no business like show business—where even a costume change is an excuse for a new marketing campaign—neither is everyone as chameleonlike as Madonna. But chances are good that the future workplace will demand similarly radical metamorphoses. It won't just be today's MBA generalist going from line management to consulting to entrepreneurship. It will be more like today's MBA generalist switching to movie producing, followed by a stint in agriculture, before going back to school to learn software design.

> The great advantage of being in a rut is that when one is in a rut, one knows exactly where one is.
>
> —ARNOLD BENNETT,
> BRITISH WRITER,
> 1867–1931

The bottom line is that career mobility isn't going to be just a descriptive phrase anymore. Rather, it will be an essential skill every professional will need in his or her tool kit. So even if you're not hoping to change careers today—or facing an involuntary career change—it's a good idea to shadow-play these tasks. Chances are you're going to need them some day.

YOUR PERSONAL MADONNA FACTOR

Take a moment now to assess your personal Madonna factor. Who are you today? What role are you playing? Is that how others see you? Is there a disconnect—a gap—between the role you see yourself in and how others see you? What does it portend for your future?

1. Who am I? Title? Responsibilities?

2. How do people describe me?

3. How do I describe myself?

4. What is the gap between how I see myself and how others see me?

5. What does this say about possible future roles?

FINDING YOUR EXIT

Barbara Cross had never wanted to be anything other than a lawyer. Very much "her father's daughter," as everyone called her, Barbara could recite the facts of her dad's cases when she was eight years old, and she very nearly qualified to serve as his judicial clerk when he was appointed to the bench—except that she was still in high school. She, of course, did brilliantly in law school, was hired by the firm everyone longed to be a part of, was named partner at an absurdly young age, and was very soon in sole charge of the firm's intellectual property practice, which she has since built into a powerhouse recognized throughout the industry.

Now forty-three, at the very apex of her profession, widely respected, immensely successful, and performing at her absolute peak,

Barbara finds it almost impossible to admit that she no longer loves what she is doing—in fact, that she no longer cares about it at all. And having thought of nothing else but a career in law since the age of eight, she has absolutely no idea of anything else she might do with her life.

She is also scared. This career has been her home, the work first and foremost, but also the particular practice she manages, the firm, the people, the office, the trappings, all

> Sometimes you wonder how you got on this mountain. But sometimes you wonder, "How will I get off?"
>
> —JOAN MANLEY, U.S. PUBLISHER QUOTED IN THE *WASHINGTON POST*, APRIL 8, 1979

of it. At forty-plus, it isn't easy to pick up and leave home—especially if you have no idea where you're going.

What's more—and by no means to be dismissed—Barbara is accustomed to the income she earns; it is a part of the value she places on herself, and it is hard to think of relinquishing it.

And there's something else: How would it look? How would it look to her family, friends, clients, and everyone else, that Barbara Cross the lawyer, Barbara Cross, "her father's daughter," Barbara Cross who has eaten, drunk, and thought about nothing but being a lawyer for twenty years suddenly wants out?

Yet "out" is precisely what Barbara wants—only she doesn't have a clue how or where to begin.

THE "ABAT" PROCESS: IF YOU COULD BE ANYBODY, DO ANYTHING . . . ?

To "get off that mountain," you begin where you always begin, where any good manager begins any decision-making process: by collecting and assessing data. This time, however, the issue is your career, and the data you are collecting and assessing concerns your abilities, talents, interests, flaws, and feelings. The process will thus require a real wrench away from subjectivity, and we've provided some exercises to help you be as objective as possible.

TASK 1: DO A REALITY CHECK: WHAT IS THE GAP?

Start this task by looking back at your personal Madonna factor chart and analyzing the gap between how you see yourself and how others see you. What is the gap between your view of you and others' view of you? Write it down here:

What do you *want* others to see in you? Spell it out:

Now, what is the single worst thing about your career right now? Write it down here—just one thing:

Keep these realities in mind as you continue the work of Task 1.

ABAT: *Any Body/Any Thing*. It's shorthand for a key question we ask people we're trying to coach and/or recruit for key positions: If there were no restraints or restrictions, nothing holding you back, no qualifications whatsoever, so that you could be anybody in the whole world and do anything at all, who would you be and what would you do? Answer this question now—both the what and the why.

Maybe you'd like to be Cleopatra—clever, with clear objectives, fulfilled, powerful, beautiful, and charismatic. Why not? Go ahead. Write it down.

And maybe, if nothing were stopping you, you'd really like to be an actor—free and uninhibited, receiving the instant gratification of applause for your talents and achievements, having the fun of playing many parts. Go for it as you fill in your personal ABAT chart:

MY PERSONAL "ABAT" CHART

1. Who would I be? (Past/Present/Future)	Why? What do I desire in that person's life or character?
2. What would I do? (Past/Present/Future)	Why? What is the passion I feel for this career?

Now expand on what you've learned from doing your personal ABAT chart. In today's world, what attributes, talents, and experiences could you bring to being the person you would want to be and having the career you would have if you could be anybody and do anything? This is a self-assessment that can tell you a great deal about how to jump-start a possible future direction—in both your career and your life.

JUMP START

My Attributes:	What other roles could I play where these attributes would be applicable and/or useful?
My Talents:	How could my talents be used elsewhere—in another position, role, or company?
My Experiences:	What I can do with these experiences in another line of work?

PROFESSIONALLY DARING, PERSONALLY RISK-AVERSE

Doug Barber had managed the IT departments of three large and successful companies and was now managing his fourth. He had assumed and hoped that each upward and forward move would increase his sense of satisfaction in his work, but just the opposite had happened: every step up took him farther down the slope of indifference. Doug was in demand in his industry and in IT and did not lack opportunities to make a job change; he had also entertained feelers from other industries, from the nonprofit world, and even from totally different kinds of work, but he had shut the door on all of them. Doug thought his dissatisfaction meant there was something wrong with *him*—after all, he was a success at a good job in a growing field—and hoped some coaching from Bill might help him see the light and gain a sense of satisfaction about this career.

The first thing Doug said when he walked into Bill's office was, "I don't want to talk about my dreams." There was a near sneer in his voice, as if he hadn't come for touchy-feely nonsense but for some straight talk, businessman-to-businessman. "I'd just like to know why I'm not feeling more content with my success."

"That's why," Bill answered. "You've answered your own question: you may not want to talk about your dreams, but clearly they're important." Not talking about his dreams didn't make them go away; it just made Doug dissatisfied with a "success" that did not align with those dreams. Instead, as Bill told him, "You're living someone else's idea of success, so it's no wonder you find your professional life unfulfilling."

Why not talk about dreams in the same breath as career goals? In Doug's case, it was clear that following his dreams held some risk for him. "You're scared," Bill told him bluntly.

Doug argued that he took risks all the time in his business decision making and therefore could by no stretch of the imagination be thought of as "scared." He was no coward, and he offered lots of assertions to prove it. He took a risk every time he outlined a course of IT development, he defensively asserted to Bill, or when he selected a development team, and on every single occasion when he spent the department's budget. In fact, Doug claimed he spent most of his time on the job assessing potential benefits and potential downsides and then choosing to accept a certain level of risk.

But as Bill pointed out, daring in the office does not necessarily equate to daring in life. You can be a bastion of courage when it comes to taking a risk on your professional success and a bundle of nerves when it comes to risking your personal comfort zone—not to mention your own happiness. So when Bill suggested that Doug consider the life risk of a career change, approaching it with as much planning, precision, and care as he brought to his professional decisions, Doug was willing to try.

> If you don't risk
> anything, you risk
> even more.
>
> —ERICA JONG

Fear can blind you to opportunities, as the saying goes—and that's exactly what had happened with Doug. But you can break through the fear by understanding what constitutes an opportunity in your terms and according to your own values, passions, and desires. Here's an exercise that will help you look for and identify your own definition of an opportunity.

TASK 2: ANSWER: HOW DO YOU DEFINE "OPPORTUNITY"?

Take a look at these components of a career. How much does each of them count with you?

THE OPPORTUNITY: WHAT DO I REALLY WANT FROM MY CAREER?

After you have ranked what is most important in Column 1 (with 1 being important), do a reality check of what you are actually getting from your current job in Column 2 (1 = what you are getting most; 14 = what you are getting least).

	COLUMN 1 Rank in Order of Importance to You 1–14	COLUMN 2 Reality Check of Current Job 1–14
Title		
Money		
Recognition		
Personal impact		

	COLUMN 1 **Rank in Order of** **Importance to You** **1–14**	**COLUMN 2** **Reality Check** **of Current Job** **1–14**
Content of work		
Status and power		
Collegiality with co-workers		
Positive office environment		
Location		
Job security		
Artistic rewards		
Community involvement		
Work/Life integration		
Feeling of self-fulfillment		

THE CURRENT REALITY: WHAT DO I REALLY HAVE IN MY CAREER?

Compare the two columns: importance and current reality. The closer your scores, the more in line your current reality is with what you really want out of your career. If more than half of the numbers in Column 1 are significantly different from those in Column 2, it is probably time to move on.

You now have a good idea of will constitute an opportunity you will pursue. Granted, this does not point you to an industry or profession; for that kind of direction, you do need to consult your dreams, your particular life passion, and your personal enthusiasms. But the self-assessment exercise you've just done should outline for you what kinds of things you should be looking at and what you (a) want to pursue, (b) are willing to accept, and (c) will not accept in your next career. In other words, when the opportunity shows up, you should now be able to recognize it.

So take the next step and jot down your top five priorities in a career versus where you are now vis-à-vis those priorities. Think of it as a portrait of your dream and the distance you have to go to realize it—a good reminder to keep returning to.

MAKING A CHANGE? HAVE A SAFETY NET?

We'll call him Carter. He was a man with a charismatic personality, a wonderful way with people, and a passionate love of learning. It was no wonder he was attracted to the training profession and succeeded at it so brilliantly. In his midthirties, he was named head of global training for a major manufacturing concern, and his bosses gave him a tremendous amount of autonomy and the resources to build the department.

There was nothing about his job that Carter disliked. He was devoted to his staff, was comfortable in the environment, and was proud of his compensation package. And while Carter cared nothing for trappings, he did love the work of training, and he was gratified by the impact he believed he was making.

Yet he felt himself trapped on the inside of that traffic circle, going around and around, concentrating solely on maintaining speed, unable to find a way out. It wasn't that there was anything wrong with the career he had chosen, loved, worked hard and succeeded at. It was that inside himself, Carter had changed course. Impacting people's lives through training was a wonderful thing, but it was no longer the thing he wanted to do. As a younger man, Carter had toyed with the idea of entering the ministry. At the time, the excitement of corporate life and the potential for personal success on what seemed a large and dramatic stage won out. Now, in his late thirties, that deep-down desire had risen to the surface. Carter still loved to teach, but what he wanted *today* was to inspire people, not just equip them with needed skills.

But such a change in direction was going to mean a huge cut in salary and benefits—and a huge adjustment in lifestyle.

Task 3: Lay the Groundwork

Any career change requires a number of adjustments, which is why you need to take time to prepare a safety net before you jump. Moreover, concentrating on the safety net helps focus your mind on your future and away from the disheartening dissatisfactions of the present. So, bottom line, what are the things you must take into consideration as you lay the groundwork for a career change? In other words, what should the safety net consist of?

1. *Money!* First and foremost, your safety net must hold money— enough to give you and your family a cushion in case you flounder or, as is possible, fail. How much is enough? The rule of thumb is to have on hand savings constituting a year's current income at the least. Two years' income is better. The more money there is, the more time you have—and time, of course, is another key component of the safety net.

2. *No Debt.* In addition to building up the kitty, try to make yourself as debt free as possible. Talk to your financial planner about ways to lower your mortgage or other commitments without losing potential tax benefits. Having to make those monthly or weekly payments can drag you down at a time when you want to be as free-floating as possible.

3. *Family Buy-in.* While money, time, and freedom from financial obligations are the most obvious facilitators of career change, they are not the only ones. Your spouse or significant other, children, friends, and relatives will also be affected by the change in your life. Carter's wife and children, for example, were effectively

being asked to undergo a major lowering of their lifestyle, a substantive rethinking of their role in the community and how they might be perceived by their peers, and a complete reversal of the family schedule—from weekends together to "It's the weekend, and Dad's working." Clearly, your safety net must include buy-in by those nearest and dearest to you. Carter's family understood and was glad about the change. It made his safety net exceptionally strong.

4. *Personal Commitment.* Make absolutely sure about your own passion for this change. Be clear that you have evaluated the options carefully, that the new career is the one you want, that you have a chance of success in it, and that you are ready. It's fine to be scared, but it's not fine to be unprepared or only somewhat committed. Commitment counts, and passion is its foundation.

TASK 4: TURN TO MENTORS AND FRIENDS FOR IMPORTANT ROADSIDE ASSISTANCE

As we'll be saying to you over and over in this book, at road sign after road sign, *you don't have to face this alone.* In fact, you probably shouldn't. As with every worthwhile and substantial endeavor, it makes sense to hear other viewpoints and get input from a range of perspectives. As always, it is helpful to find a mentor.

Start with your friends. The fact that they like you doesn't necessarily mean they won't tell you what they think. Some, to be sure, may argue against change in your life because it means a change in theirs, but you should be able to cut through that and get to the real issue.

Of course, we may be prejudiced, but a move this big is worth some professional guidance as well. Janice says she often sees people who have achieved enormous success in their current careers, yet simply cannot see the next opportunity; she helps them do that. Bill, too, coaches many business executives who don't seem to be able to think of their career as a business—subject to strategic planning and tactical decision making; he shows them how. That's what professionals do: help you analyze your skills, interests, and opportunities and refine your thinking so that you're moving in the right direction.

Be it friend, professional, or objective third party, a mentor can help keep you on track—especially through the rough patches that are bound to occur. And he or she may also be able to offer substantive help—especially when it comes to networking.

THE PLAN

Sally saved her money, got the blessing of her husband and children, asked her friends and colleagues to start networking on her behalf, and on a Friday in October, walked away from the director of marketing job she had held in an insurance firm for sixteen years—free at last to pursue a new career. The next night, she, her husband, Jack, and their dearest friends went to dinner and drank a bottle of champagne to celebrate Sally's "new beginning."

But on Monday morning, with Jack at work and the kids in school, Sally burst into tears. She had no office to go to, no agenda to follow, no purpose to her day. She had made no plan for how she would embark on finding a new career, and despite all her business skills, she had no idea what to do.

Sally's failure is your object lesson, and it is Task 5 of the process:

TASK 5: MAKE A PLAN
It's astounding how often the most accomplished corporate managers—meticulous planners when it comes to the company's goals, resources, and capabilities—simply fail to carry out this most fundamental management task in their own lives. It is enough of a wrench to leave the "home" of a career; to leave it blindly, however, is downright foolish.

Sure, you can contemplate leaving one career without knowing with absolute certainty what the next career should be. And even if you do know what you're going to do next, you may not be sure how you're going to do it. Even if you know that, you surely won't know how or whether your career swap will work. But no matter the situation, you need a plan to do it.

Here is where a professional career development coach could have helped Sally, although anyone who has worked in corporate America ought to have some idea of how to create a basic plan. For Sally, who had no idea what to do next—except that it couldn't be marketing and it couldn't be in insurance—the components of such a plan could be as simple as this:

A BASIC CAREER CHANGE ACTION PLAN

POSSIBLE EXITS TO TAKE

1. Market Opportunities: What is available for the position(s) I seek? Companies in Area: Positions Advertised:
2. Network: Whom do I know who works for these companies or in similar positions? People: Positions:
3. Conferences: What conferences can I attend to see if that is the position I truly want?
4. Whom do I know who can help me get the job I want? Friends/Family Members: Agencies: Search Firms: Ads:

Had she had such a plan on paper, Sally would have known precisely what to do Monday morning; she would have been dry-eyed, on the phone—and on her way to a new career.

TASK 6: TAKE SIDE TRIPS: EXPLORE THE TERRAIN OF POSSIBILITIES

There really is a world of other career and job possibilities out there, and it can be immensely helpful to drive over and check some of them out. So take some side trips to other industries and other jobs to see what other folks do for a living and whether their road of choice is one you might like to follow.

Naturally, it may not be possible for you to shadow another professional at his or her job to observe what it might be like. Only movie stars get to be a fly on the wall of real-life workplaces other than their own.

But you can certainly identify volunteer activities or freelance possibilities in which you can test what other kinds of work are like. (In fact, you can often do this while still at your old job.) Is the publishing industry a possibility? Volunteer for the PTA's newsletter. Are you interested in health care? Hospitals need all kinds of volunteer assistance: offer your local health-care center your high-level management skills, or work as a gofer helping patients; both will open your eyes to a different industry and way of life. Considering marketing? Get on a local committee, charity, or company project to promote a community event.

Simple things can introduce you to all sorts of people and all kinds of new and different ways of making a living. Whether you live in a big city or small town, agree to run the local holiday parade or set up a vendor's table at the street fair. There are street fairs from New York City to Iowa City—and everywhere in between—just about every weekend of the spring and summer. Far too many street fairs, in fact. It isn't that you expect or hope to land jobs like the one you've volunteered for at your local street fair; rather, you're widening your perspective and thus stimulating your thinking about possibilities for your own next career.

TASK 7: EXECUTE

The time does come when you simply must make the change. If you've done the six previous tasks in the process, you should be well placed to do so successfully—whether you're making the change of your own volition, or you are being pushed.

If you have assessed honestly why this career no longer works for you, have defined your own idea of an opportunity so you'll recognize it when you see it, have stitched up a safety net, have received some mentoring, have written a plan, and have opened your eyes to the wide-ranging possibilities in the world of work, then you're ready to reinvent and renew yourself and your profession.

Go!

SUMMARY

Sometimes a career really does stop working for you. Don't get trapped; get out. Here's how:

1. Self-assess. Do a reality check: What is the gap?
2. Define the "opportunity" for you.
3. Lay the groundwork.
4. Turn to mentors and friends for important roadside assistance.
5. Make a plan.
6. Take side trips: explore the terrain of possibilities.
7. Execute.

Don't Be Burned Out, Bummed Out, Unfulfilled: Strategize a Way Out of the Dead-End Career

Janice: There's nothing worse than being dissatisfied with your job. You spend at least a third of your life at work, and if you're trying to make a career for yourself, you spend much more than that in effort, energy, and commitment. For so much of your life to be boring or unfulfilling is such a waste of a life!

Bill: Unfortunately, for reasons of necessity, inertia, or complacency, people accept the boredom as a way of life. We get so accustomed to lacking fulfillment that it becomes a habit. We lose the dream we once had of a life's work that could be fulfilling—enriching in many ways. That can be a very numbing thing.

Janice: When you've been running on empty for so long, you forget what it's like to have a tank full of positive energy. I see this problem in so many people in the corporate world today, particularly in women—middle-aged Baby Boomers and even Gen Xers—and it's the cause of a real brain drain out of corporate organizations.

Bill: The trick, I think, is to recognize the signals before you run out of gas altogether and bump up against a career dead end— with no gas station in sight.

THE DEAD-END CAREER

On a flight out of St. Louis, Charley Simmons and the young woman sitting next to him, an IT executive at a well-known financial institution, start up a routine work-related airplane conversation. Then the young woman goes off-script. She asks Charley, "Do you ever feel you've lost your sense of direction? That the whole thing has just come to a screeching halt? I do. I even wrote it down in my personal diary. Look." The young woman taps her BlackBerry, and there it is on the calendar, like any other business appointment. She is thirty-five years old, she tells Charley—ten years younger than he— and she feels burned out, unable to see or feel a future for herself.

The shock of recognition is potent. The young woman has articulated exactly what Charley Simmons feels: that his career is at a dead end. Psychologists call it *career depression syndrome*. They're finding it not just in the downsized, the insecure, and those waiting wearily to retire, but in young people and those at what should be the peak of their careers as well—individuals with theoretically exciting job assignments that come with all the trappings of success. No one is entirely certain about the reasons for the syndrome, but its signs are clear: a feeling of dissatisfaction, decreased motivation, low confidence, dwindling competitiveness, self-doubt, self-criticism, and a lack of clarity concerning goals.

Charley Simmons embodies the syndrome perfectly. A relationship manager par excellence, whose way with clients was so renowned that he was featured in a B-school case study, Charley now drags himself from airport to airport, not sure which city he is in or where he is headed next. There was a time when he couldn't wait until the flight attendant announced that it was OK to use laptops; Charley would flip his open and peruse the notes in his contacts files again and again, plotting how he would reach this next prospect, mentally composing the package of services to sell him, strategizing how to parlay one contact in a company into several. Now he just naps through the flight—and still can't figure out why he is so exhausted on arrival at his destination. Where he once swaggered into meetings with prospects, he's now nervous dealing with even his best clients, worried that he has forgotten some key detail, unsure if they're going to fall for his proposal.

For all his travels, Charley no longer knows where he is going. He can't remember his career goals—or if he ever had any. Without a clear vision, there's nothing to exercise Charley's imagination or arouse his enthusiasm; he's utterly bored. He vaguely remembers the passion he once brought to his work, and he is puzzled as to what that passion was about—and where it went. He feels that his career is heading up a blind alley toward a dead end, but he can't seem to muster the energy to change direction. Maybe he thinks there's a career air bag that will keep him from crashing. Or maybe he just doesn't care anymore.

What about you? How much do you still care? Is excitement about work a distant memory—and are you nostalgic for the feeling? Are you heading up that blind alley that Charley Simmons is traveling? If you are, we've got to get you out of there *now*. For one thing is certain: if you can't get past the Dead End sign, the next seventeen signs really will not matter.

TASK 1: FIND OUT *NOW* IF YOUR CAREER IS HEADING FOR A DEAD END

What's wrong with your career? Why do you feel you are caught in a blind alley, going nowhere fast? Maybe the organization you're in has simply ceased to be "home"—a place where you feel comfortable and appreciated, an environment that inspires you to give your all. Or maybe it's actually the work you do—the content of your assignment. Sure, it's work you thought you wanted to do once, but maybe the nature of the work has changed—or maybe you have. Either way, it is no longer a turn-on and no longer fulfilling.

Here's a test that will address these issues and help you figure out if your career blind alley is a matter of where you work and/or the work you do.

The first set of five questions addresses the organization you're in and will let you know if you're even on the right road—that is, in the right place for a fulfilling career. The second set of questions will help you determine if it's the content of the job itself that may have you heading for a dead end. Answer each question with scrupulous honesty, and then add up your total score.

IS IT THE ORGANIZATION?

	Always 1 point	Frequently 2 points	Occasionally 3 points	Rarely 4 points	Never 5 points
1. Do you wake dreading the day ahead and being in that company and culture?					
2. At the end of the day, do you feel that your accomplishments do not "fit in" with what others in the organization are doing?					
3. Do you find that the people with whom you interact at work are difficult and not supportive?					

	Always 1 point	Frequently 2 points	Occasionally 3 points	Rarely 4 points	Never 5 points
4. Does the company devalue what you are doing and openly demonstrate its lack of interest in you?					
5. Do you sometimes need to take a "mental-health day"?					

TOTAL SCORE: _____

For the questions you've just answered, 1 through 5, the higher the score, the farther away you are from that dead-end street. Here's how it breaks down:

If you scored . . .	It means you . . .
20–25	pretty much like where you are and where you're going.
15–19	are reasonably satisfied with your career highway.
10–14	should probably take the test again in six months.
5–9	may be headed toward a dead end.

Now it's on to the next set of questions, those addressing your view of your work itself. The results will indicate to you if you're in the right position.

IS IT THE JOB—THE WORK ITSELF?

	Always 1 point	Frequently 2 points	Occasionally 3 points	Rarely 4 points	Never 5 points
6. Are most of your tasks and responsibilities things that you love doing?					
7. At the end of the day, do you feel invigorated by what has transpired?					
8. In discussing your work and career with family and friends, do you feel proud of what you are doing?					
9. Is what you are doing an accurate reflection of who you are and what you enjoy?					
10. When you are alone, do you say or think to yourself, "This is exactly what I want to be doing"?					

TOTAL SCORE: _____

For these questions, 6 through 10, the lower your score, the better. Here's the breakdown:

If you scored . . .	It means you . . .
5–10	are riding high.

If you scored . . .	It means you . . .
11–15	are OK for now.
16–20	may be starting down that blind alley.
21–25	need to act fast to avoid the crash.

In addition to noting your point scores, also take a solid look at the content of your answers. What does it tell you if, for example, you answered that you *rarely* feel invigorated at the end of the workday? Or that you only *occasionally* find the people around you enjoyable and supportive?

Ask yourself if you feel dissatisfaction with the direction and pace of your career, how confident you are of your own competence, whether you suspect that your career has lost its way, if the daily grind has grown stale, and if a look forward to the rest of your career brings up a picture of an arid, tedious stretch of leaden days. If so, you're heading for a dead end.

Make sure, however, that it isn't some other aspect of your life that is affecting your feelings about your career and not the other way around. Be honest with yourself. Dig deep. There may be dead ends in other parts of your life as well.

In any event, these two exercises should tell you if your career problem is due to the organization you're in or the work you do—or both. Hold the thought; you'll need it by the end of this chapter.

BOREDOM BOULEVARD

Mary has been in the accounting profession for sixteen years—and nobody does it better. Still, sixteen years of doing the same thing day in and day out had gotten to her, so eighteen months ago, she looked for a new opportunity. Several quickly presented themselves—Mary's particular expertise is highly desired in any organization—and she chose the one that promised an easy commute, the best compensation, and a liberal set of perks.

But eighteen months later, Mary is as bored in the new organization as she was in the old. Nothing about the new job is stimulating. Yes, she has a fresh set of office furniture and nifty engraved business cards. And yes, she is working with new people—well, they were new eighteen months ago. But she is still doing the same thing she has always done. She does it so well it has become a trap. "You can do this stuff in your sleep," people tell her admiringly. But *asleep* is exactly how she feels . . .

DEAD-END DIVERSIONS

Do an Internet search on "bored at work," and the search engine returns more than 2.4 million links—mostly to sites that provide humor, games, and chat rooms that let you talk to other bored people. Maybe you've been there yourself . . .

Let's find out. Be honest with yourself as you answer these questions:

1. When do you feel at your best?
    - Morning, on arrival at work
    - Lunchtime
    - Afternoon/evening, on leaving the office
    - At the bar, hoisting a few before taking the train to go home after work

2. You're working hard, trying to concentrate, when suddenly you're interrupted. Does the interruption . . .

- feel welcome?
- irritate you?
- not affect you at all?

3. Do you find yourself putting off crucial decisions?

4. Is it tougher and tougher to actually sit down to start work?

5. Do you care?

Bottom line: Are you driving on Boredom Boulevard—or are you already parked there?

Either way, it's time to get off.

For Mary, the first step to getting off Boredom Boulevard was to realize that she had put herself there and kept herself there. Among the new job offers eighteen months back were opportunities to relocate, to travel, to help a start-up enterprise. She had turned them all down to "stick with what I know and am comfortable with."

Eighteen months later, in her annual performance review with her supervisor, she uncharacteristically spilled the beans that she was bored, and she asked her supervisor about "other opportunities."

"Other opportunities?" her supervisor repeated, stunned. "Didn't you see them?" He ticked them off: the invitation to join a strategic task force that she had spurned because it sounded like a lot of work, the chance to make a presentation at the investor relations conference that she had turned down on the grounds that public speaking made her nervous, the possibility of joining the deputy CEO's team for customer visits that she had thought, ironically enough, sounded "boring."

No, she hadn't seen these opportunities. She was driving her career highway with blinders on, looking neither left nor right. In fact, she could barely see past her dashboard. It was time for Mary to risk an abrupt, sharp turn of direction.

Mary's kind of blindness doesn't happen overnight. It accumulates in small increments until the work turns into mindless habit, and the environment seems like wallpaper you no longer need to look at. You'll have to break the habit and rip off the wallpaper if you're going to exit that endless turnpike to tedium and get your career back on track.

Task 2: Explore Other Job or Career Opportunities

Really?

Of course. Why not? At least start looking. Do it today. Open your eyes to possible opportunities right in your own organization, which, like virtually every organization, no doubt has a Job Offerings bulletin board next to the elevator or on the company Web site. Talk to people about these opportunities. Find out what each possibility might entail, what the job content is, and what its future potential could be. You'll be surprised to find that the simple act of exploring can lead to entire new worlds of options.

Then look outside your company. Attend a conference or meeting concerning a job, industry, or career you have thought might be of interest—even if the thought has been way back in your mind. Then talk to people about it. Suppose you're a marketing manager—a bored marketing manager. Maybe public relations would be interesting—or maybe you're just clutching at straws. To find out, attend a conference on PR. Drop in on a range of sessions to get a feel for what the profession entails. Talk to conference attendees. Do these conversations get your juices flowing?

Now that you've opened your eyes to the idea of a change of direction, keep going. Make a list of those other possible positions in your company and write down why they might be good for you. Make a list of the outside meetings you could attend that would teach you about alternative job or career possibilities. Note the times on your calendar, and task yourself to meet the deadlines for signing up.

The point is action; simply moving an inch can unlock the tedium in which you've been driving on cruise control down Boredom Boulevard. That inch alone can show you that there *is* another road, and that you *can* get there from here.

THE PASSIONLESS POTHOLE

Given his reputation as a mover and shaker, the line and staff people reporting to newly hired Dave Michaels were surprised at his cool, distant demeanor and passive behavior. Dave was a little surprised himself. He thought he would show up at the new job, knock a home run as he always did, and tip his hat to the crowds applauding on their feet as he rounded the plate. But the truth was that this time, he just didn't seem to have the same hunger he used to have. At meetings, he felt himself zoning out, thinking more about the new house he and Sarah were building in the mountains, wondering if the kids, soon to be on their own, would really visit them there. Although he dutifully tried to bring his mind back to the matter at hand, he felt no urgency about whatever was being discussed and began to question whether it mattered very much. The excitement he used to feel in meetings like this—the adrenaline high of working out a high-flying deal he knew he could achieve—seemed a distant memory. He was drifting—and it showed. No wonder he never saw it coming when they fired him.

Is the zest gone? Maybe your career was going along nicely— until suddenly your front wheel went down into the passionless pothole, where it spins and spins aimlessly. Or perhaps you never felt the passion that causes people to look forward to going to work in the morning, makes them eager to take on assignments, interact with colleagues, assume new challenges, show what they can do. Yet unless you can go at it with gusto, what's a career worth?

Do any of the following describe you?

- Low motivation
- Minimal effort
- Just "treading water" and trying to stay out of the line of fire
- Little initiative
- Lowered self-confidence

If you're suffering any or all of these symptoms, your career has very likely fallen into the passionless pothole.

Is passion essential in a profession? Absolutely. No, we are not meant to live in a perpetual state of exhilaration, but we are also not meant to live without passion. A job that never stirs our enthusiasm or our emotions is just a job, not a profession. It is, moreover, a job at which you cannot, in the end, succeed. Without passion, performance must suffer; you're just spinning the wheel, burning rubber while your tires continue to lose traction.

TASK 3: REFOCUS TO RECLAIM YOUR PASSION

Dave had a long way to go to climb out of his passionless pothole. At first, he kept reaching for the kinds of highs he used to feel, but duplicating the old deal-making situation didn't bring a duplicate passion.

He and Sarah moved into the country house, and at her urging, Dave got involved in the local community's efforts to preserve an eighteenth-century farmhouse. He found that his talents and experience could make a difference in the campaign—and were valued. And he found that he valued the effort. The experience lifted him up high enough to climb out of the passionless pothole.

Dave couldn't replicate his old passion—he had lost it some-where along the way and couldn't find it anymore. But by reaching outside himself to refocus on an external goal, he could tap into the long-banked passion he had once known—and could reclaim his zest for action.

Here's an exercise that will help you refocus your way out of the passionless pothole:

Think back in time and focus in on a single great "high" in your professional life. What was it about that situation, incident, or event that exhilarated you?

Now examine your world today. What situation or event or person or even object provides you a feeling that most resembles that past moment of passion? Is there something or someone that can help you create *another* high—not necessarily the same as before, but a similar intensity of feeling? What can you do—specifically—to bring this feeling back into your current situation?

You can't copy your old high, but you can look for a context or set of circumstances that will stir your engine once again—so that you can ignite your way out of the passionless pothole.

RUNNING ON EMPTY

"These e-mails are eating me up," Howard complained. "There aren't enough hours in the day . . . Impossible to do it all." Robotically, he worked his way through the e-mails, the FYI Post-its, the clippings, the meetings. He had always been known as a guy who could get a prodigious amount of work done, and while he still tried to do it all, he found that little was being achieved. "Too many interruptions," he protested. "Can't delegate this," he insisted. "This has to come from me." In meetings, he sat and stared; when asked his views, he tended to offer a lecture that was just a bit off the point. "I'm exhausted" was his mantra, at work and at home, where he would simply flop down in front of the TV. He didn't seem to notice that it was as out of focus as he was.

He only knew he felt depleted, with nothing left to give to the job or the company. And he wondered how long it would be before senior management noticed and sent him packing.

Does this sound like you? Maybe, like Howard, you're just going through the motions. Your personal workload seems overwhelming, your personal skills seem overtaxed, and the whole concept of "motivation" has become a joke. By the end of the day, you're pretty sure that one more e-mail or one more ringing phone will put you over the edge, and when you get home from work in the evening, all you want to do is collapse into mindless inertia. Even the weekends aren't sufficient to recharge your batteries, and your family has begun to complain that you're not spending time with them; you're just marking time.

Worst of all, you can't see the purpose of the work you do, which may be why no one seems able to tell you if you are doing it well.

Are you running on empty?

Take the test below to find out.

RUNNING ON EMPTY?

	Rarely 1 point	Sometimes 2 points	Frequently 3 points	Always 4 points
Do you know what to focus on at work?				
Do you know what to focus on in your personal life?				
Do you feel physically well?				

Do you know what makes you feel down?				
Do you take time just for yourself—i.e., to think, meditate, exercise, etc.?				
TOTALS:				

Now total up your score and analyze the results:

If you scored . . .	It means . . .
16–20	your tank is pretty full; you're on a smooth ride.
11–15	you are about three-quarters full; is there a leak?
6–10	look for an energy station; you need to fill up.
5	you are empty; it's time for professional roadside assistance.

If you scored anywhere below 20, you will need to stop at an energy station to refill your tank. The lower your score, the more frequently you'll need to stop and the bigger the refill you need. But it isn't just the size of the needed refill; it's the quality of it that counts.

THE PRESENTEEISM PROBLEM

A 2003 study estimated that depression on the job costs employers $44 billion a year in lost productivity (and costs depressed workers untold millions more in direct medical costs). The $44-billion price tag for lost productivity isn't because depressed workers are absent. On the contrary. It's because they are present—but functioning at depressed levels. The problem of presenteeism includes missed deadlines, failure to return phone calls, indecision, lateness, lack of cooperation, troubled interaction with colleagues, poor-quality work, too-long lunches, and too-early departures. These depressed workers are there, but they're not there; they're at work, but they're not working; they're on the job, but they're not doing the job . . .

Howard knew there was no more juice left, and he knew the company would simply let him go if he had no more to offer. He wouldn't blame them; they were paying him good money, and he was no longer worth it. He just had no idea how to restore himself.

He figured it out at 37,000 feet. It was a late-afternoon flight filled with corporate executives, like him. He could tell they all were because the minute the flight attendant announced that it was OK to use electronic equipment, laptops snapped open up and down the plane cabin. Their screens lit up, and the familiar icons flickered to life.

And suddenly Howard thought, *What on earth are we all doing? This flight is two hours long. Can't we pause from business for that long?* That's when it hit him: *Can I pause from business for that long?*

He could—and he did.

When he got home that evening, Howard called his pastor and asked to meet with him. Over the next days and weeks, he concentrated on spiritual replenishment. It helped him sort through what counted and what didn't. Then he set about forcing himself, in both his life and his work, to focus on what counted and let go of what didn't. It left time for reflection and for a life beyond the office. He got to know his family again, reactivated his habit of morning jogging, gave himself permission to devote weekends to play, and felt his brain clearing and energy seeping back into every facet of his life. He learned that chilling out is filling up, and that stepping back is a good way to put positive energy back in the tank.

TASK 4: REFILL YOUR TANK WITH POSITIVE ENERGY

Pull up to the pump, turn off your motor, and get ready to refill your tank. Here's how:

Tip 1: Sit for ten minutes doing absolutely nothing but thinking. How does that feel? Chances are it feels good.

Tip 2: Make a list of what you have done for others on a personal, one-on-one basis.

For example, maybe you have coached a child—your own or someone else's—or worked with the underprivileged, or offered your business or organizational skills to a local civic organization, food bank, amateur theater group, blood drive, etc. If there is nothing on the list, Tip 2A would be to get busy. (If you are doing a lot, your tank is probably pretty full already.)

Tip 3: Take a look at the books on your bedside table. Now put aside those that have to do with business and those that are sheer entertainment. Instead, go get a book meant to inspire you. Read it.

But that's not all. Talk to others about it. If you weren't inspired, try to figure out why. What might other people recommend instead?

Tip 4: Go learn something new.

If you're not learning, you're standing still. And if you're just relearning the same old stuff, no wonder your tank is empty. So go take a sculpting class. Study art or music appreciation. Sign up to learn a foreign language. Do something educational for yourself—something not connected to your profession, something for the sheer sake of learning.

TASK 5: DETERMINE WHETHER THE DEAD END IS IN THE ORGANIZATION, THE JOB, OR YOU YOURSELF

Back in Task 1, you assessed the nature of your career dead end—whether it was due to the organization itself or to the content of the work.

If the problem is the organization you're in, it's an understatement to say that your ability to influence organizational change is limited. Most of us drift down the highway, hoping that we will be discovered within the organization, appreciated, and therefore promoted. We're sorry to tell you it simply doesn't work that way. That doesn't mean you must give up on the organization altogether. It does mean you need to come at the problem from a different perspective. Here's how:

1. *Gain all the information you can about how the organization is doing and where it's going.* Can you fit here? Is there a role you can play in influencing which way the organization will go or the direction it will take? Your power to do so may be limited, but limited doesn't mean nonexistent.

2. *Explore every opportunity to examine what's going on right around you—and assess what it may mean for your job security.* Unfortunately in today's world, rumors too often become fact, so it's essential to probe beneath the rumors. Is your division doing poorly? Is the overall organization not performing to expectations? If you sniff a lot of negativity in the air, chances are it's there, and if it is, be assured it will impact you one way or the other. Job loss happens; believe it, and start looking for other opportunities outside the organization before it happens.

3. *Study your boss.* Try to get as close to him or her as possible to ascertain what is going on. You have a right to inquire about other opportunities and about where the boss sees the company going. And make sure you listen with an objective mind to what the boss says. Keep in mind that a division or position you would

not have considered in the past may be your ticket out of a dead end today, and since the boss is the one who may have the answers on the subject, don't be afraid to ask: "Is the opportunity there? Is it real? What would it take for me to capitalize on it?"

Sound aggressive? Let's call it "assertive," and let's remember that most organizations like their executive talent to be aggressive. Keep in mind that those who do not show an interest in improving the organization tend not to be rewarded for long—if ever.

4. *Keep your finger on the pulse of opportunities outside the organization on a regular basis.* The concept of corporate loyalty is dead. No one is loyal to you—except you. You can demonstrate that loyalty to self by making sure you have the right skills and attitude to contribute to your current and future organizations as you ride *your* career highway. In fact, we think you have a moral obligation to look after yourself and your career—always with sensitivity toward the welfare of the organization that pays you and the feelings and interests of those you work with.

> No matter how much pressure you feel at work, if you could find ways to relax for at least every hour, you'd be more productive.
>
> —DR. JOYCE BROTHERS

Nevertheless, the obligation to yourself includes keeping an eye on the market and having an updated résumé always at the ready.

If the problem is the work *itself*, that requires a different set of actions. Can you, in fact, change the nature of the work you do? Yes. Here's how to get started:

Identify the three things you dislike most about your job, and try to diminish or eliminate those activities.

Identify the three activities you like most about your job and see if you can expand those activities—thus building on your strengths—to have a greater influence on the organization.

Ask your supervisor what you need to do to contribute more to the organization. Are there skills you should improve? Learning you should undertake? Organizations you should join? Anything you can do that will at the same time help grow the organization *and* advance you along your career highway is an essential driving tool. Go get it.

Here's a template to help you map out a new approach to your organization and your job:

Expand: Increase What Maximizes Your Interest and Enthusiasm	Diminish: Decrease What Minimizes Your Interest and Enthusiasm	New Opportunity Within the Organization	New Opportunity Outside the Organization	Who Can Help

But of course, as the self-assessment exercises of this chapter may have taught you, the problem may be in neither the organization nor the job but in yourself—because of where you are in your life at this time.

Here are some ways to bring yourself back from a career dead end when *you* have created the dead end:

1. Reach out to others. Do something that gains you no personal return.

2. Take a week off to think about you.
3. Discuss your situation with friends, family, and mentors.
4. Start an exercise program.
5. Seek professional guidance. There can never be any shame associated with this; it represents strength, not weakness. If you're up against a dead end on your career highway, you just may need roadside assistance from professionals who have dealt with dead ends before. Ask them for help.

TASK 6: TAKE THE PLEDGE, MAKE A PLAN, AND THEN EXECUTE

We never said it would be easy. As with most things in life, once you've analyzed yourself and explored all the solutions, only you can implement the change. That's why we encourage you to "sign up" right here to your personal plan—three action steps are all you need—for avoiding the dead-end career.

THE PLEDGE

I will undertake the following three action steps to improve my current dead-end situation and get out of the blind alley. I also commit to sharing my plan with at least one other trusted person, and I will ask that person to hold me to my action plan. Here's the plan:

THE PLAN

1. _____

2. _____

3. _____

Now turn your car around and get out of that blind alley and back on the fast-track highway to your career goals.

SUMMARY

When your career is stuck in a blind alley and about to crash into a dead end, take the following actions:

1. Find out *now* if your career is heading for a dead end.
2. Explore other job or career opportunities.
3. Refocus to reclaim your passion.
4. Refill your tank with positive energy.
5. Determine whether the dead end is in the organization, the job, or you yourself.
6. Take the pledge, make a plan, and then execute.

Avoid Being a Victim:
Mobilize the Power Within You

Janice: There's a virtual epidemic these days of people who feel absolutely powerless in their careers. They act like the proverbial deer in the headlights: blinded, rooted to the spot, motionless.

Bill: You are so right. People have lost initiative and energy. And they blame it on the boss or an unhappy personal life or 9/11 or some other external.

Janice: It's understandable. People have been through so much— so many mergers and acquisitions, consolidations, downsizing. They're in a state of near-constant worry over what's next. It paralyzes them.

Bill: They've lost control. It's a victim mentality.

Janice: Well, in your coaching practice, how do you coach people out of victim mentality?

Bill: It starts with them realizing that they *can* have control and that they *must* get in front on the issue. It's about taking responsibility for their destiny.

DEER CROSSING AHEAD

Casey Martin woke up at 2 a.m.—again. This time, she was certain she had gotten the date wrong on the invitation to the museum event. For the next four and a half hours, she lay rigid on her back, her eyes wide open, staring at the darkness, while Bob snored rhythmically beside her.

The night before, she had awakened to worry about a limo for the celebrity talent highlighting the event. The night before that, it was whether the podium microphone was sufficiently adjustable for the foundation's powerful but very short executive director.

Casey had only taken on the museum event because the culture at the foundation expected you to assume responsibilities outside your own "silo," as the executive director put it. Now the event was taking all her time, while her "normal" load of deadlines still loomed. The real problem, however, was that none of it was much fun anymore. It was just worry that kept her from sleeping.

A month ago, driving home from the office, Casey had set the cruise control to 60 and tried not to think about work. A sudden flash of white up ahead made her slam on the brakes—hard. There, in the headlights, was a terrified deer: legs splayed on the highway, eyes wide but unseeing, unable to move forward or back. *Which of us is more paralyzed?* Casey remembered thinking. Which of us is really more likely to be run over—the frightened four-footed animal, or the midcareer woman who feels stopped in her tracks and powerless to do anything about it?

WATCH OUT! ARE YOU BECOMING A VICTIM?

It's a fair question—and more and more professional people are asking it of themselves these days. If you're asking it, it's probably because you feel trapped, inadequate, and absolutely unable to do anything about it.

How can you? You don't control the economy—which today is unlike anything any of us has ever seen. We have jobless recoveries, inflation-prone recessions, and global dependencies no one has quite yet figured out. Neither the top economists nor the Las Vegas bookmakers have been able to predict what's next for the economy, so how can you possibly know what's coming?

You can't control your boss either, or his boss, or the company you all work for. Mergers, moves, downsizing, rightsizing, all seem to happen at the whim of a few CEOs who talk only to one another or, worse yet, to themselves! Whether it's method or madness, it begins to be a huge chess game, and no matter how important your job or how big your budget or how vast the army of people you manage, you're really just another pawn. (Note: remember that even CEOs are pawns these days—with an average tenure of three to four years before they take that golden parachute, are disgraced, and/or float out of sight.)

And as just another pawn in the great corporate chess game, you've had to take on extra responsibility because (a) two other divisions were summarily downsized, or (b) the culture, as in Casey Martin's workplace, "expected" it, or (c) you figure it's the best way to get ahead. Only you're not getting ahead. You're not getting anywhere. In fact, your productivity is down, and, like Casey, you have missed or are about to miss deadlines.

And how does all this make you feel?

There's one big problem with feeling like a victim: you start acting like one. And when that happens, you have let yourself become powerless. You have given up control of your career and your life. When you act like a victim, you really are ready—as Casey Martin was—to be run over, steamrollered, and absolutely flattened by the very next car to come down the career highway.

BEING IN NEUTRAL

There was a time when you had control, but right now, you're just idling in neutral. Where did the control go? Did someone take it away? We often give up control and allow ourselves to become victims when we feel so overwhelmed we would just rather let someone else take responsibility—or when we feel so inadequate that we don't think we're capable of making decisions.

So consider first how, why, and when you lost control—just when it was that you allowed yourself to become a deer in the headlights.

TASK 1: FIGURE OUT HOW YOU GOT STUCK IN NEUTRAL
Kick off this task by writing down the answers to these questions:

In what situation did you lose or relinquish control?

When?

How did the loss of control or decision-making power feel?

Did you like letting someone else call the shots?
Yes _____ No_____
Explain:

If you could take back control, what would you do?

Did someone else take control? Make an inventory of
people who have controlled you—and assess how they
managed to do that.

People Who Have Controlled You / How They Controlled You
1.
2.
3.
4.
5.

If you want to, what can you do to take back that control?

GETTING BACK IN GEAR

Ted was forty-five years old with twenty years at one of the world's
most prominent corporations. At a time of life when most men
expect to feel in their prime, Ted was simply scared stiff. All around
him in the great complex that was his company, men and women
of every age and length of service, at every level of the hierarchy, in
every function and possessing every skill, had been demoted, relocated, or summarily terminated. There seemed no rhyme or reason
to it. As Ted saw it, the message was clear: if it could happen to
these people, it could happen to him.

Ted hoped that coaching from Bill might give him some sort of
advantage, although he conceded to Bill that he felt he was "just
hanging on" in his career, had ceased to learn anything new, and
was no longer pushing the edge of the envelope. Just like Casey
Martin, Ted came up with the deer analogy: "I feel I'm stalled in

the headlights," he told Bill. "It's like I have no control whatsoever over whatever might be coming at me."

That's when Bill asked the key question: "When did you last feel you had control over your career?" The question momentarily stumped Ted, but when he began to reflect, his entire demeanor as well as his reply indicated he was just beginning to see outside the blinding lights.

The truth is that even posing the question is the starting point for regaining control. That's why it is such a key task for getting out of the deer-in-the-headlights trap in which you find yourself.

TASK 2: REMEMBER AND REPLAY CONTROL SO YOU CAN GET IT BACK

Here is an essential exercise for getting back the control you once had:

> Think back to the last time in your professional life that you really felt in control. If you can't find anything in your professional life, then think about your personal life. Was there a time or moment when you felt you really held your fate in your hands? Whether it was holding your own in a discussion in a college seminar, or helping win the game at summer camp, or making that presentation to the executive committee when you felt you were clicking on all cylinders—what was it about that situation or incident that gave you that feeling of control? Think about it; then write it down here:

> What acknowledgment or recognition of your control did you receive at that time? Write it down.

By now the goal should be clear: to regain the kind of control that brought that acknowledgment.

STOP COMPLAINING
AND START LISTENING

Janice once tried to recruit a woman we'll call "Marie" for a particularly important, powerful, and attractive senior-level position. She had heard about the candidate from one of Marie's former coworkers, who reported that when they worked together years ago, Marie had complained constantly about her job and the company. Janice was surprised to hear that Marie was still at the company and assumed it was because she was afraid of being out of work. But since Marie had precisely the right background and credentials, Janice felt pretty confident about approaching her for this new, exciting position.

She was completely surprised when Marie thanked her for calling but said she had no intention of ever leaving her company.

"But the word was that you were fed up years ago," Janice said.

"That's true," Marie admitted. "I was fed up years ago, and for a long time—actually, for the first seven years I was here. But of course, I was too afraid to make a move."

"So what changed?" Janice asked.

"Somebody began telling me I was doing a good job," Marie said. "The company started to promote me—this is after seven years on the job. My supervisors started giving me high ratings and publishing my work. Once I felt I was actually achieving something, I could achieve even more. And now I have a name in the marketplace; I am so well recognized in my field that I'm simply not ready to make a move." She added: "Tell my former coworker, by the way, that I've stopped complaining."

One good way to regain control is to stop complaining and start listening. Listen to your own complaints, for starters. What messages do they carry? Typically, complaints reflect unmet needs, unrealistic expectations, or festering problems. In each case, you can do something about it. You can create an action plan to meet your needs. You can rethink expectations that have no chance of being fulfilled. You can solve problems instead of letting them go from bad to worse.

You can also listen to what your circumstances and environment are telling you. In the example above, Marie didn't have to wait—paralyzed by fear—to take action. Sitting around for seven years before finding out that she was doing a good job says as much about her passivity as about the company's inadequacy in reviewing its employees. She could have asked how she was doing, explored how to do her job better, taken action on her own behalf.

As we said at the very beginning of this book, no one cares as much about your career as you do, and no one is more obligated to take care of it than you.

Task 3: Create Your Initiative Inventory

Have you spent a lot of time complaining? Or worrying? Or blaming the economy, your coworkers, your boss, your CEO, or the movements of the planets and stars for your current trapped feeling? Maybe, as it was for Marie, it's time to start listening to what's *right* with your career.

Go back through every job you've ever had—anytime, anywhere—and create an inventory of the initiatives you have undertaken that have paid off. What did it feel like when something you initiated worked? What made it work—i.e., what were the elements of your own abilities that made the initiative happen and succeed? Write it all down here:

Your Initiative	Your Feeling	How It Worked	What Made It Work?

Chances are, you had to overcome some obstacles to make the initiative succeed. What were they? Check off the relevant obstacles in the following list. And remember: you overcame every single one of them.

❑ Self-Esteem ❑ Peer Acceptance
❑ Self-Confidence ❑ Family Approval/Acceptance
❑ Inadequacy ❑ Fear of Failure
❑ Other:

LOOKING PAST THE HEADLIGHTS, GETTING OUT OF THE TRAP

You have now established that you are capable of some control over your career, and you have analyzed the abilities you possess that constitute that control. You have overcome the obstacles and recaptured the initiative that you once had. You've learned that you don't have to be a victim—and that victimhood happens only with your consent. So how do you break the paralysis that's keeping you blinded in the headlights right now? How do you climb out of this trap?

TASK 4: ASK YOURSELF: WHAT ARE MY TRUE EXPECTATIONS?

Start by analyzing your true expectations and seeing how they match up against reality. Here's an exercise that will help:

	Always 1 point	Frequently 2 points	Occasionally 3 points	Rarely 4 points	Never 5 points
1. Do you expect/want someone to take care of you and bail you out?					
2. Do you feel unable to take control and assume responsibility?					
3. Do you constantly look to others for praise and seek their approval?					
4. Do you feel inadequate— less capable than others?					
5. Do you repeatedly ask others for advice and not trust your judgment?					
TOTALS:					

If you scored . . .	It means . . .
20–25	you are not in a victim trap. Congratulations!
15–19	you're well positioned to climb out of your trap.
10–14	you need to ratchet up your sense of yourself.
5–9	time for a reality check: you are in a victim trap.

Here's the truth of the matter: no one can take care of you. Even if someone who loves you is "taking care" of you, he or she cannot take care of your ability to control your career or your life. Only you can do that.

Task 5: Make a Contract with Yourself: You're Not Going to Be a Victim Anymore

Just decide: "I am in control; I am no longer a victim." It is the best way we know of to get yourself in gear and moving forward.

How do you do it? Fill out the following contract, copy it, hang it on your refrigerator, and imprint it on your mind. The very act of writing out the contract is a way of taking control.

CONTRACT

I, [YOUR NAME], hereby proclaim that I am not a victim and that I am in control of my own destiny. I further pledge and agree:

1) that I will not allow others, such as

_____, to make decisions for me;

2) that I will not allow situations of the past, like the following,

_____

_____ to repeat themselves;

3) that I will not allow myself to feel inadequate or bullied as I did in the following situations:

_____

_____;

4) that I will accept responsibility for my own well-being as I did in the past, as in the following situations:

_____

_____;

5) that I will again take control as I did in the past, as in the following situations:

_____

_____.

(signed)

THE PAYOFF

Even getting a finger over the edge of the trap is empowering, enhancing your sense of control and cutting through the first layer of the victimhood onion. The subsequent layers will peel off easily as you climb higher. Soon enough, you'll find that your feet aren't rooted to the spot after all. In fact, they're ready to move you forward.

SUMMARY

When you're the deer in the headlights where your career is concerned, do these things:

1. Figure out how you got stuck in neutral.
2. Remember and replay control so you can get it back.
3. Create your initiative inventory.
4. Ask yourself: What are my true expectations?
5. Make a contract with yourself: You're not going to be a victim anymore.

Reinvent Yourself: Be Prepared for Stuff to Happen!

Bill: In filling positions, how do you assess whether candidates are prepared for the unexpected curves every job has?

Janice: It isn't easy, yet *continuously* preparing for change is one of the most important attributes anyone can bring to a position. I look for candidates who have shown resilience and who coped with the change. They didn't whine; they coped! You can't always anticipate the unexpected, but you can always try to make yourself more valuable.

Bill: Sounds oddly familiar. Be prepared when opportunity knocks —or you get knocked.

Janice: The only sure thing is that there will be curves up ahead, and there's no telling how sharp they will be or in which direction they will bend.

Bill: To navigate the curves, hold on to your job and career, and be viewed as a valuable player to the company, you are almost certainly going to have to reinvent yourself again and again.

A WINDING ROAD

The merger was announced on a Tuesday morning, with a bland statement about "significant personnel reductions" buried in paragraph five. To Tim Pearson, the announcement sounded like the start of a race, with his career as the prize. Yes, he did an essential job for the company, and he was very, very good at his job. But essential as he was, even a larger, merged institution probably only needed one person to do it—and that meant that Tim and his counterpart in the other merging company, whoever he or she might be, were in a contest starting right now. This was a new reality that entirely upended all of Tim's expectations about his career; it signified adjustments to his personal plans and family life and, quite frankly, shook him to his core.

Julie Ralston walked out of her performance review reeling. To say it had not gone well was an understatement. She had expected a good conversation with her boss—an objective and analytical look at her achievements and misses, a rigorous discussion about what had produced the former and led to the latter, a meticulous assessment of how to take matters forward. Instead, she was subjected to a real dressing-down. What she thought of as "misses" were failures in the company's eyes—and it seemed it was these failures that defined her. In one hour, Julie's professional life had changed drastically. Her future looked bleak, and even her present situation seemed iffy. The floor under her feet suddenly felt shaky.

Stuff happens. No career highway runs straight and smooth. All roads have curves, and curves can be unnerving to the driver. Any profound change in your work situation—a demotion, termination, merger, acquisition, relocation, even a promotion—can plunge you into a state of fear, anxiety, depression, anger, or mistrust. Like Tim and Julie, you feel as if you have sustained a hit and can't quite feel your tires on the road.

You can't avoid these emotions, nor should you. Loss must be experienced. Fear and anxiety must be acknowledged as real feelings and dealt with, sometimes with the help of a professional. So don't beat yourself up for having these emotions. Feel them. Experience them. Let them happen. But don't let them knock you off the highway.

Let's face it: the economic reality of the early twenty-first century does not offer the Tims and Julies of this world many assurances. Mergers typically mean that somebody wins and somebody loses. And given the vast pool of talented individuals looking to be hired, even one bad performance review can be the handwriting on the wall. But those who can manage the curves coming at them, navigating the twists and turns, who stay in control no matter how winding the road, and come out the other side still in control of the car, are the ones who will succeed.

The bottom line, therefore, is to prepare yourself for the curves ahead. Just as on any highway, decelerate before you enter a curve to make sure you are in control. Then, at the midpoint of the curve's arc, accelerate to grip the road and come out of the curve at normal speed. It's tricky, but it works!

But the key question remains: How do you prepare yourself for what you can't be certain of down the road? You start now. Long before any sort of curve appears, ready yourself for the possibility of twists and turns ahead so that you stay in control. That's how you'll take the curves safely, and that's how you'll keep yourself on the track of your career highway.

TASK 1: LOOK AT A MAP: SEE HOW THE ROAD WINDS AND TURNS

Driving the steep mountain passes of the Alps of southern France can be nerve-racking, as Janice can testify personally. Starting out, she had eagerly anticipated following the scenic route over the mountains—"a marvelous adventure," the guidebook had said. Then came the steep inclines, narrow roads, sheer drops, and hairpin curves—with no guardrails!—that made the drive an unforgettable test of skill and mental endurance. Janice remembers gripping the wheel so tightly that at the end of the three-hour ordeal, her hands had deep nail marks. The only saving grace was her friend and navigator extraordinaire, Heidi, who accurately read the map and signs so that Janice could anticipate the terrain and adjust her driving accordingly. No wonder there were so few cars on this "scenic route"; it was for experienced drivers only—experienced drivers who could read a map and follow signs in French!

Fortunately, for the most part, there are signs on the corporate highway too—and it's a good thing, because that highway, like the alpine route Janice drove, can be treacherous. In any organization, however, even basic research can help you map the organization's topography; see how the road winds; and navigate its twists, turns, and curves. Such research will also give you warning signs of the subtle shifts and drifts that may be indicative of more seismic changes ahead. If you can't ascertain exactly what those changes might be, at least you'll have a hint that they're coming.

Following is an exercise that will get you started on that kind of research. It's a monitoring operation you should do routinely, on a very regular basis, whether you suspect there's something going on with your company/job or not. Just as your local radio station updates you on traffic conditions every ten minutes, you need to update your company's potential curve conditions every month or so.

The chart recognizes that in every company, changes are going on all the time: Senior management has meetings with investment bankers. Analysts of companies talk about how a merger of equals

HIGHWAY CURVE CONDITIONS

Are There Activities That Suggest This?	Yes/No	How Might It Impact Me?	Is It a Plus, a Minus, or Neutral to Me?
Merger/Acquisition			
Reputation Risk			
Being Acquired			
Downsizing			
Restructuring			
Reorganization			
IPO			
MBO			
Being in Play			
Being in Trouble			
Chapter 11			
Scandal			
Stock Price Issue			
Getting a New Board			
Getting New Management			
Poor Sales Picture			
Poor Bottom Line			
Other			

could yield greater gains than the separate entities achieve on their own. IPOs are being planned—though an offering may be put off repeatedly or, in the end, not done after all. Divestitures are being contemplated in boardrooms and back rooms. And talk about just being bigger or better than the competition is an ongoing conversation—the corporate leaders' mantra—for good or for ill. Stuff is happening, and the better you can keep tabs on things, the better chance you have of knowing about it before it happens, or at least being better prepared.

Looking at the chart, start by finding out whether anything in the left-hand column is going on in your company now, or is being contemplated, or may be contemplated soon. How can you find this out? You must have friends in other areas of the company—and if you don't, find some. You can also listen and watch. Keep your antennae up, and keep your eyes open as you observe the activities around you. Explore the terrain—and be on the lookout for warning signs and directional signals.

There are other ways to dig out news around the corporation. Log on to the Web site once a day if you can, and see what news corporate HQ has put on the home page. Be sure to check out the press section to read the latest press releases. Stay current on the CEO's major speeches, which are typically archived on the Web site, and don't neglect the corporate financial statements. Is your company's quarterly earnings report typically reported on cable TV? Be sure you see it.

But don't stop there. Do an Internet search on the company name and/or on the CEO name and see what comes up. Is there gossip or speculation about corporate plans or company personalities? Listen to the rumors; after all, they may be true. How is the company perceived by others? Search engines can often lead you to a treasure trove of information, rumor, guesswork, or analysis you won't hear in the hallways.

Once you've checked yes or no to the possible twists and turns the company may be going through, figure out how each twist or turn might impact you—both directly and indirectly. Is the IPO something you can take advantage of? In a merger, would your department be the winner or loser? Could a new management team mean a new opportunity? Once you've determined the nature of the potential impact, rate whether it would be positive, negative, or neutral. Assess the number of negatives and see if you might be in a troubling situation.

At the end of the exercise, you should have a good idea about where some possible curves up ahead may take you. It's important information, but make sure you don't immediately react to the potential impacts. Remember: it's essential to decelerate before a curve; that's how you keep control. Think about what may be ahead. Think about the potential impacts. But keep your speed at a manageable level, and keep a firm grip on the steering wheel.

DECELERATING BEFORE THE CURVE

Jim had long assumed that he was in the direct line of possible successors to the CEO—until he had a substantive, intimate talk with a member of the board of directors and learned that he was behind others on the road. Realistically, with the blinders off, he was so far down the line that he had no chance at the top spot. In fact, he had gone about as far as he could go at the company, where he had invested twenty-eight years of his career, and he was unlikely to rise much higher. The news was a crushing disappointment, and Jim *felt* crushed—weighed down, reduced in size, utterly defeated by this unexpected downward bend in his career.

One night while Jim was licking his wounds at home, an executive recruiter phoned him to talk about a position with another company in another field altogether. The position was both attractive and challenging, and in an instant, Jim felt hopeful and energized. But it presented him with another curve—this one an upward spiral into an unknown territory where he had not traveled.

What Jim did *not* do was just react. Although it was midweek, he and his wife, Betsy, packed the car full of food and wine and headed up to their weekend place in the mountains. For a couple of days, they ate good food, drank good wine, took long walks, and talked of everything *but* Jim's dilemma or the future. With a clear head, Jim began an in-depth analysis of both of the options before him—staying where he was in the sure knowledge that he would rise no higher, or answering the call to engage in a new job in new territory and test himself. He looked at each in terms of challenges, risks, costs, and benefits, trying to create a framework within which he could make a clear assessment and a wise choice. The new position offered an extremely attractive financial package along with the challenge, both exciting but a bit daunting, of starting an entirely new learning process at ground zero. The old job held no more challenges to rise higher, but it did perhaps offer a challenge to contribute more deeply in an area Jim knew well and enjoyed.

Over the weekend, and with Betsy's help and support, Jim continued to sharpen the analysis and hone the possible scenarios—until finally it seemed to him to come down to a choice between money and the satisfaction of making a contribution he was supremely well qualified and experienced to make.

In the end, it was no contest. Jim chose to stay on at the company he knew and loved. He was content not to become CEO at the company—and not to make more money than he could ever spend at a new company—because he believed he could make a difference in a unique and important way. He had taken a look around the curve; what had first seemed the greenest of pastures now looked dull, and what his anger and depression had at first painted as a bleak landscape looked like a rewarding place to call home. Two years later he was named CEO of his company. Life throws a lot of curves.

TASK 2: MEASURE YOUR HORSEPOWER: DO A SKILLS INVENTORY

OK, you've mapped out what may lie ahead and how you may be affected. Now you need to assess your potential for dealing with what's coming. In a nutshell, what level of horsepower—skills, attributes, experience, and accomplishments—do you bring to the issue of navigating the curves ahead?

SKILLS INVENTORY

Most-needed skills in organizations today fall into these categories:

Basic skills for learning or for acquiring knowledge:
- Listening, critical thinking, communicating

Interpersonal skills for working with people to achieve goals:
- Negotiating, influencing, service orientation

Problem-solving skills
- Decision making, analysis, troubleshooting, judgment

Functional skills
- Finances, marketing, operations, risk management, technology, compliance

Management skills
- People coaching, relationship building, communication

Execution with excellence
- Conceptual big-picture design
- Visionary
- Leadership
- Strategy
- Tactical

Following is an exercise that will help you see what skills you have—and what skills you need. When we talk about skills, however, we are not just talking about the ability to crunch numbers or manage a project. Your functional capabilities are or should be a given. Nor are we talking about such "softer" areas of expertise as being "good with people" or being "a strategic thinker." Certainly, those are good strengths to have.

> Prosperity is a
> great teacher;
> adversity a greater.
>
> —WILLIAM HAZLITT,
> ENGLISH ESSAYIST,
> 1778–1830

The key here, however, is to possess skills the company *values*. And while all companies give lip service to the basic skills, you can tell which ones it truly values by looking at those who have succeeded in the company: the skills they are known for are the skills this company prizes most. So Step 1 is to size up the skills the company values. Write them down in Column 1.

Then determine objectively and fairly whether or not you possess these skills. If not, how feasible is it for you to obtain the skills needed? Finally, where you lack a valued skill that is feasible to obtain, set down a method for obtaining it. That means putting in place a procedure for acquiring each of the skills you'll need to successfully navigate any sharp curve that may be thrown at you.

MEASURE YOUR HORSEPOWER

Skills the Company Values	Yes, I Have This Skill/No, I Do Not	Obtaining the Skills I Need Is Feasible/Not Feasible	How Can I Obtain These Skills?
1.			
2.			
3.			
4.			
5.			

The deliverable of this exercise should be a single action plan for souping up your horsepower to meet the likely curves in your own personal career highway. Now you have to follow the plan.

TASK 3: GET A DETAILING JOB: REINVENT YOURSELF

Car detailing is a meticulous and often tedious job. It requires special equipment, special oils and waxes, and special techniques. And it is comprehensive—from the basic washing to removing the seats to rinsing the engine, claying the finish, and doing the final touch-up.

You'll need the same fastidiousness when it comes to reinventing yourself. Execute your plan from Task 2: go get the skills you need. Maybe you'll have to sign up for a course, or transfer to an area in the company where you can learn the skill on the job, or "apprentice" yourself to a mentor who can help you learn the skill outside the regulation hours and requirements of the job. Do you lack real expertise in marketing—in a company where marketing is the be-all and end-all? Hook up with some of the marketing stars; watch how they do it, and follow where they lead. You're not replacing your engine; you're making it more powerful.

You may need to take multiple actions to master a single skill. Gaining financial proficiency, for example, may require asking questions of the controller, poring over the MD&A (the Management Discussion and Analysis, as auditors call it, of the company's financial conditions and the results of its operations) of your company's annual report, reading a book like *Finance for Dummies* or taking a course in the subject, or all of the above.

Whether one action or many, the key is to have a *specific* plan with targeted dates for each action. Here's a model self-reinvention plan; fill in the blanks:

REINVENTING YOURSELF

Skills Needed	Specific 3-Step Action to Acquire the Skill	Target Dates
1.	1. 2. 3.	
2.	1. 2. 3.	
3.	1. 2. 3.	
4.	1. 2. 3.	
5.	1. 2. 3.	

TASK 4: TAKE A TEST DRIVE—AND HONK YOUR HORN TO GET ATTENTION

On the strength of a single presentation, Georgia was selected to run an entire division. She was not prepared to meet this upward curve in her career, and she knew she would have to reinvent herself fast. To do so, she took courses and was given a coach—Bill Morin, in fact. She also changed her hairstyle and her wardrobe, bought a new car, and assumed a more confident style of behavior.

The old Georgia was everybody's pal, a shoulder to cry on, a colleague you could chat with endlessly. The new Georgia had little time for any of that; her division-head role required a whole new way of relating with others. Bill showed her how to let her warm personality shine while not letting others take time away from her new responsibilities. Georgia learned to refer to herself as being in Georgia High-Gear mode when she sensed it was time to cut off an interaction and move the car forward.

To show she fit her new position of leadership in every way, the new Georgia exhibited a trait she learned from her coach: she raised her finger whenever she made a decision. It was her way of showing that she had taken responsibility for that decision—and let's move on. But Bill also coached Georgia how to do this with style and, whenever possible, with some humor.

In the same way, when you have done the detailing job on your career vehicle, honk your horn to let people know you're brand new and have heightened horsepower. After all, there's no point in reinventing yourself if no one knows or believes it. To show you are prepared for whatever may happen, look like it. Let your external appearance and behavior mirror the internal reinvention you executed in Task 3. Show off what you've got and what you've done. If you have developed a keen ability in marketing, be part of the team that drives the look and substance of the annual report—and let the folks who count know you contributed. If you have taken a course in computer technology, speak up at the next IT meeting to make it clear you understand the issues involved in developing a needed piece of software—and maybe you have a solution to offer. Be visible, take a stand, and be sure to listen as well as communicate your point of view—always in an appropriate way. Let the other drivers know you're there, prepared, and ready to take every curve on the road and come out at top speed.

SUMMARY

Every career highway has its twists and turns, any one of which can stall your progress, stop you in your tracks, even send you careening off the road. Prepare yourself for the inevitable sharp curves ahead by doing the following:

1. Look at a map: see how the road winds and turns.
2. Measure your horsepower: do a skills inventory.
3. Get a detailing job: reinvent yourself.
4. Take the new you out on the road—and honk your horn to get attention.

Adapt: Fit In or Find a New Road

Janice: When assessing people's fit with their company, what do you see as critical for staying on the career highway—critical for making sure they don't get derailed?

Bill: No question about it in my mind: the ability to adapt to the culture and operating style is the most crucial element for staying on track. As in evolution, those creatures who adapt survive. The dinosaurs failed to adapt to climate change and went extinct. I know an awful lot of managers who very nearly went extinct because they failed to adapt to a merger or a new market or even changes in the sales approach.

Janice: Absolutely. Evolution is a perfectly apt metaphor. In a corporation, the way of life is a changing environment, and the fittest survive in the environment because they adapt to the culture as it changes. And change it does—constantly!

Bill: I can hear the dinosaurs screaming. Too bad they didn't have a road sign. Yield is a sign everyone will see on the career highway, because if an organization is not changing, it's probably going to die. So, too, for the individual in that company.

THE ROAD SURFACE
CAN DETERMINE THE RIDE

In an era of instant communication delivered in bits, bytes, and vivid graphic images, the XYZ Corporation stubbornly clung to what it liked to call "our way of doing things." "We like being stodgy," the CEO proudly proclaimed, and the most iconic manifestation of that stodginess was the legendary Monthly Briefing Book delivered to the CEO on the first Thursday of every month. Housed in a red three-inch ring binder, The Book, as it was routinely called by those who produced it, typically contained anywhere from six hundred to eight hundred pages of charts, graphs, lists, and plenty of narrative copy detailing virtually everything that had gone on in XYZ the previous month.

As chief of staff, it was Larry Hodges's job to get The Book produced, to deliver it personally, and to present its information in a briefing that began at 7 a.m. and never ended before lunch. For Hodges, an organizational wizard who had come to XYZ from a highly successful technology research consultancy in a laid-back university town, the ten days or so preceding delivery of The Book were a nightmare. The CEO liked his information cut every which way—except the way Hodges thought made the most sense—so Larry put in endless amounts of time riding herd over a bunch of number crunchers, then sitting up till all hours with the graphics people around a high-resolution screen, figuring out the best way to show the data, then overseeing the actual "manufacture" of the required four copies of The Book for the CEO, CFO, COO, and CIO, plus a fifth for himself.

One Wednesday, when Hodges had been at XYZ only ten months, as he left the office at 10:30 for the ninth night in a row, having personally punched holes in the final one hundred pages of the final copy of The Book because headquarters was out of three-hole paper, he passed the open door of the CFO's chief of staff, Ted Loomis. "Half day again today?" Loomis joked as Larry walked by. It was standard witticism at XYZ, where long hours were the norm, but on this particular night, it set Larry's teeth on edge. In that moment, the in-joke seemed to him to symbolize everything about XYZ that didn't fit who he was: the vaunted stodginess, long work-days as evidence of commitment to the job, the formal structure. There was nothing wrong with any of it, and certainly XYZ was a fine organization that offered important products and services to an eager market. But, as Larry suddenly realized, it just wasn't *him*. It wasn't his style, didn't match his personality, and constituted a culture in which he simply wasn't at home. And although he had a good job with a promising future, to Larry Hodges, the cultural disconnect seemed reason enough to leave.

The next day, he polished up his résumé and called the head-hunters.

MOVIN' ON AND MOVIN' OUT

We hear the term *corporate culture* so much we tend to forget what it means and how important it is. To begin with, it means the very same thing it meant when you took Sociology or Anthropology 101: the sum total of behaviors, social patterns, beliefs, institu-tions, traits, and thought products particular to an organization. By definition, therefore, corporate culture determines what it will be like to work in the organization—what your life will be like as a member of such an organization. It's the road surface, and it determines the kind of ride you have on your career highway.

That's why it is so important. A job may be just the assignment you've always wanted to have, may provide a great salary and bene-fits, and may offer plenty of room for advancement, but if being there day after day feels to you like a very uneven road surface, or if it seems to be tearing up your tires, or if your vehicle rides too low to miss the speed bumps, even the best job in the world will become oppressive—and you could end up wrecked by the side of the highway.

We both have personal experiences of being in the right job in the wrong culture. Unwilling to adapt to cultures that didn't fit us—and into which we did not fit—we both solved the problem by leaving the organization.

Janice found herself in a corporation known for being consensus oriented and highly bureaucratic, a place rich with opportunity for achievement, but where such achievement came in a very structured, formulaic way. To Janice, this simply felt "boring" and "not entrepreneurial enough for me." After five years, she moved instead to a fast-paced financial institution where wallflowers, yes-men, and the risk averse simply did not fit in. She had to be on her toes every second, because she never quite knew what was coming next. Yet she felt entirely at home in that particular culture—nourished by it. For her, it offered an exciting ride to success.

Similarly, Bill once landed in a well-known firm whose hierarchical structure felt like a straitjacket. Fresh ideas were not unwelcome, but they took a long, long time to work their way up and through the hierarchy. He soon broke out of the straitjacket to form his own consulting firm—and influence the corporate culture from the top down, determining the road surface for himself.

The truth is, founding your own firm is about the only way you can really change a corporate culture, for trying to go up against established norms of behavior and institutionalized rituals is almost always doomed to failure. Iconoclasts may get mentioned in the history books, but it is usually because of the futility of their struggles.

That's true in business too. Carly Fiorina, the much-vaunted onetime chair of Hewlett-Packard—whom we'll meet again when we get to Road Sign 15—was the square peg in a round hole at HP,

much as it needed her square-peg style. Appointed CEO to shake up the legendary firm, known for its brilliantly innovative founding and its reliance on imagination, Fiorina's numbers focus and rigorous style clashed with HP's style of doing things—and led to her eventual downfall. She shook the place up all right, and it thanked her by

> Adapt or perish, now as ever, is nature's inexorable imperative.
>
> —H. G. WELLS, BRITISH WRITER, 1866–1946

getting rid of her. The pundits even hypothesize now that Jack Welch stayed too long at GE, till the culture he had implemented needed its own rebellious iconoclast.

No. Trying to single-handedly transform the rituals and style and personality of an organization is a recipe for failure. You cannot change it; it will change you, or you will leave. Survival comes through adapting. Triumph can come through adapting particularly well. And as with the dinosaurs, failure to adapt to your corporate culture can mean extinction.

MOVING THE SIGN

But culture is an organic thing; it moves and grows and changes all the time. It has to, for just as no road surface lasts forever or remains unaffected by traffic, weather, and other forces, no corporation can stand still in the face of a changing economy, market shifts, technological innovation, and personnel turnover.

The merger is perhaps the most common reason for paying attention to the Yield sign—at least in our shifting economy, where innovation so often breeds consolidation. Janice tells of a candidate she was recruiting for a large manufacturing firm that suddenly merged with a competitor midway through the recruiting process. Under the terms of the merger, the CEO of company A became the CEO of the merged company, while the CEO of company B became the COO of the merged company. Suddenly, a lot of people would not be reporting to the person who hired them. Suddenly, a lot of jobs would be changed or eliminated. Suddenly, two fairly disparate cultures would have to work as one. And suddenly, Janice's candidate announced he'd like to slow down the recruiting process until he could have a better idea of the culture that would emerge and of the impact it might have on his career. "Call me in a year if the slot is still open," he told Janice. He not only yielded; he pulled over to the side of the road to see how others fared on the new road surface before committing himself to a culture where he might not feel at home at all.

On your career highway, there will often be instances where you'll want to yield so you can see how the other cars are proceeding, so you can make sure there isn't some speedster coming up fast behind you, or so you can catch your breath and settle your thinking before you proceed onto the superhighway. Keep in mind also that this is one road sign that you'll see in just about any situation and all locations. You can find it in the fast lane as well as in the slow. You'll see it at a major intersection in the center of town and on a dirt road in the back of beyond. It's telling you there's a situation up ahead that is likely to cause you some trouble, burden, thought, change of plans, consternation; get ready to adapt.

And that's precisely why you yield; so that you can prepare to meet whatever is coming and adjust your driving accordingly, whether you have to slow down, squeeze into a single lane, take a

detour, or just wait in traffic for an indeterminate amount of time—
in other words, adapt. If you cannot adapt, you need to change
direction entirely, find another road, or wait for the tow truck to
haul you away.

That's why we will present four tasks through which you can
identify the culture of an organization, assess how well you fit the
culture (and how well it fits you), determine how to adapt—if
adaptation is needed—and decide whether you are willing to
adapt or would be better off simply turning around and going
somewhere else.

GOOD AND HEALTHY

Is a changing culture a good thing? Research says it is—
emphatically.

A culture that is strong enough to be flexible and agile
can more easily adapt to market change, economic shifts,
and technological innovation. Even during an economic
downturn, the research makes clear, adaptive cultures do
better financially than those with rigid or poorly defined
cultures.

The reason is simple: according to one study based on
some 350 sources, employee productivity and retention, customer loyalty, and bottom-line results are all indelibly linked
to an organization's "cultural health."* So the healthier the
culture—i.e., the more agile and adaptive—the more productive, stable, and high-performing the corporation.

*Corporate Culture and Organizational Health, Dr. Joel Levey and
Michelle Levey.

TASK 1: DETERMINE WHAT KIND OF CULTURE YOU ARE IN

You need to understand a culture before you can determine whether or not you can live and work in it comfortably. So Task 1 is to identify the culture of your organization or one you are considering joining. We've put together a four-category matrix that will guide you in identifying a particular corporate culture.

Start with the *type* of organization it is. Classic management theory identifies four organizational types, and while many organizations are a combination of types, one type will usually predominate. Which one predominates in your organization?

- **Analytical:** a numbers-driven organization in which everything is measured, structured, subject to control
- **Driven:** a fast, open, occasionally confused organization in which getting it done is the focus
- **Traditional:** a systems-based, process-and-procedure bureaucracy aimed at building order
- **Innovative:** a risk-taking, casual organization that prizes creativity above all else

Three other categories of behavior and values further define those types: leadership style, operating style, and personality.

By *leadership style*, we mean the manner in which the organization is directed. Is it run by *royal command*—with the top leader calling the shots and everyone else falling quickly into line? Is it leadership by *collective*, with a broad-based executive working out the overall direction and subcommittees interpreting that direction down the line? Perhaps your organization is led by *consensus*, with senior management working by persuasion and negotiation to bring all ranks to a certain level of commitment to an objective. Finally, leadership by *deputizing* pushes responsibility down and down in the organization, assigning every team member full responsibility for specific tasks. Which style defines your organization's leadership?

Once you've defined the type of organization yours is and the style of its leadership, determine its *operating style*. By operating style, we mean the way things actually get done in the organization. Again, there are four basic operating styles, so choose the one that best fits your organization:

- **Open**, in which people cut across the hierarchy to network together to get the job done
- **Political**, in which people are protective of their own turf as they play to win
- **Silo**, in which discrete agendas are pursued separately and in a highly focused manner
- **Familial**, in which people work as a community or brotherhood, sharing credit and blame equally

Again, while organizations may have mixed operating styles, one style usually predominates. Identify the dominant operating style in your organization.

Finally, what is the *personality* of the organization? This is an elusive concept, to be sure, but every organization certainly has a personality—a temperament and character that distinguish it from every other organization. You feel it when you open the door of the headquarters building in the morning, or when you get off the elevator on your floor. It's in the air of the place, making it "smell" and feel like no place else.

We've categorized personality in seven either-or descriptions, one of which certainly prevails at your organization:

- **Gunslinging vs. methodical:** This is a shoot-from-the-hip place—or it's one that prizes method and precision.

- **Punishing vs. nurturing:** There's no time for nurturing here; we've got work to do—or we invest in developing talent.
- **Lone wolf vs. full crew:** I've got my job, you've got yours, and who needs a team?—or we all pull together making it work.
- **Sprinter vs. marathoner:** We don't sacrifice today's bottom line to tomorrow's possibilities—or we serve today best by simultaneously investing in tomorrow.
- **Risk-taking vs. risk-averse:** It's better to take some action than none, no matter the risk—or think before you leap.
- **Gluttonous vs. balanced:** Family values are nice, but face time at the office is what counts—or you're a better worker if you have a full life.
- **Personality disorder vs. multipersonality:** Inconsistency in policy and practices keeps people on their toes—or we're not bound by any particular set of rules.

Circle the descriptors that best match your organization.

Personality
Gunslinging vs. Methodical
Punishing vs.Nurturing
Lone Wolf vs.Full Crew
Sprinter vs. Marathoner
Risk-Taking vs. Risk-Averse
Gluttonous vs.Balanced
Personality Disorder vs. Multipersonality

Type	Leadership Style	Operating Style
Analytical	Royal command	Open
Driven	Collective	Political
Traditional	Consensus	Silo
Innovative	Deputizing	Familial

Of course, identifying a culture—deciding which descriptors to circle—is not quite like counting the number of employees in a company or listing its products or services. It requires observation and exploration that are at once more subtle and more profound than the information in the corporate brochure. So how do you determine which descriptors apply?

One good way is by finding out who succeeds in the organization and who fails—and why. Who are the car wrecks in the organization—and what caused the wrecks? Who are those people in the slow lane? What's the scuttlebutt on them—and what labels get pinned on them? Check the shoulder of the road. If it's littered with breakdowns, what is the nature of the breakdowns? Did they run out of gas, get a flat tire, or crash and burn?

Take a look in your rearview mirror. Why were those cars passed? Why are those drivers now falling behind?

Now look ahead. Who are the drivers up ahead who managed to speed away from change and are now setting the pace on the highway? How did they do it?

Many other attributes and features of an organization will also alert you to its type, leadership style, operating style, and personality. The way employees interact, the degree of competition, and the amount of sheer fun at work—if any—provide clues as to the level of pressure on people in the organization. Dress code, office décor, on-site perks, communications techniques and styles, whether there's a company picnic and a company Christmas party: all of these things will help you decide which descriptors in the matrix to circle; all are hints to the corporate culture.

TASK 2: ASSESS HOW WELL YOU FIT IN THE CORPORATE CULTURE

It's the key question: Is the organization's culture one you can commit to? That is, how much do you have to adapt, if at all, to be at home in the culture?

To help you answer that question, we've prepared a questionnaire. Mark each statement as either true or false for you:

1. ___ I enjoy working with my peers.
2. ___ I share this organization's values.
3. ___ I am comfortable with the way this organization operates on a daily basis.
4. ___ I have no problem achieving things within the framework of the organization's structure.
5. ___ I believe this is a place in which I can achieve the goals I have set for myself.
6. ___ I understand and can play by the rules of this organization.
7. ___ The teamwork here is effective and welcoming.
8. ___ There are role models in the organization whom I can emulate without sacrificing my personal style.
9. ___ I am comfortable practicing the kinds of behaviors this organization prizes.
10. ___ I believe the organization appreciates the way I conduct myself.
11. ___ I believe instinctively that, overall, this organization is a good place for me.

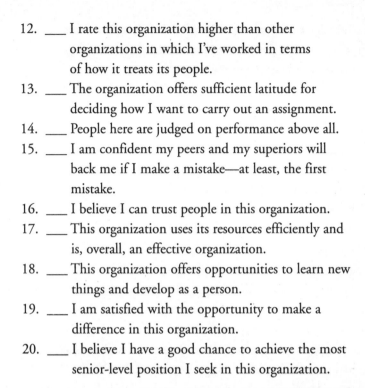

12. ___ I rate this organization higher than other organizations in which I've worked in terms of how it treats its people.

13. ___ The organization offers sufficient latitude for deciding how I want to carry out an assignment.

14. ___ People here are judged on performance above all.

15. ___ I am confident my peers and my superiors will back me if I make a mistake—at least, the first mistake.

16. ___ I believe I can trust people in this organization.

17. ___ This organization uses its resources efficiently and is, overall, an effective organization.

18. ___ This organization offers opportunities to learn new things and develop as a person.

19. ___ I am satisfied with the opportunity to make a difference in this organization.

20. ___ I believe I have a good chance to achieve the most senior-level position I seek in this organization.

If you have **sixteen** or more "true" answers, this is the place for you. Clearly, you are comfortable in the culture and can easily commit to it.

If you found between **ten** and **fifteen** statements that were true for you, that indicates a small but perhaps important adaptation gap. Turn back to the matrix in Task 1 to analyze carefully where the gap is. What is it about this organization's type, leadership style, operating style, and personality that makes you feel a disconnect with the organization? Assess how important the disconnect is; it may be too important to ignore, or it may be possible to adapt to it.

If you have **fewer than ten** trues, it is probably going to require a major effort for you to adapt to this organization. Think hard about staying here.

Finally, if you answered "true" **fewer than five** times, move on. This is not the place for you. Find another road or take another direction on your career highway.

TASK 3: FIGURE OUT WHAT YOUR ADAPTATION TUNE-UP WILL REQUIRE

Anything more than five true statements certainly positions you to adapt to the organization's corporate culture, but it's essential to know the extent of adaptation that will be necessary, what behaviors you'll have to change to adapt, and what resources will be needed to make the changes. Bottom line: you need to assess your own adaptation gap and develop a plan to close it. Your assessment should cover two aspects of the gap: the disparity between your behavior and that of the organizational drivers, and the discomfort you may feel with the type, leadership style, operating style, and personality of the organization.

Start by checking out the difference between your behaviors and those of the fast-trackers who are setting the organization's pace and managing the forward direction. Study how they operate and how they interact with others. Compare that to the way you operate and interact with others, and determine what behaviors you might emulate to enter more comfortably and successfully into the culture.

Who Is on a Fast Track? Names and Titles	Their Operating Behaviors	Their Interaction Behaviors with Others	Behaviors I Feel Comfortable Emulating

Now consider your level of comfort or discomfort with the culture as you described it in the culture matrix, measuring the gap on a scale of 1 to 10. How ill at ease are you with the type of organization it is? To what extent do you think the organization's particular leadership style is keeping you from achieving what you could? How at home are you in the organization's operating style? And how far out of tune are you with the organization's personality— i.e., how big is the gap? Measure the gap; then note the changes you would need to make or actions you would need to take to close it.

Describe Your Organization	My Comfort Gap 1–10 (Low to High)	Changes/Actions I Can Make to Close the Gap	Target Date
Type			
Leadership Style			
Operating Style			
Personality			

You're just about ready to go. But before you carry out the plan, there is one final task you need to carry out.

TASK 4: DECIDE IF IT'S WORTH IT

You understand now the culture in which you live and the actions you must take to adapt to that culture. But whether the adaptation

> The reasonable
> man adapts himself
> to the world; the
> unreasonable one
> persists in trying
> to adapt the world
> to himself.
>
> —GEORGE BERNARD
> SHAW

gap is large or small, and whether the actions required are many or few, decide first if the adaptation is worth it to you.

In terms of your own values, how comfortable are you with the changes you would have to make? How confident are you that the actions you have planned to take will mesh with your own way of doing things? If you are going to find, as Larry Hodges did, that the culture just sets your teeth on edge, it would be preferable to create a plan for getting out rather than for adapting to an unyielding culture where you will simply never be at home.

SUMMARY

Corporate culture isn't a sideshow; it's a persistent and unyielding fact of the environment in which you work. It cannot be dismissed. You must either continually adapt to its changing nature—or change direction and find another road to your career goals. To determine which course is right for you, do the following tasks:

1. Determine what kind of culture you're in.
2. Assess how well you fit in the corporate culture.
3. Figure out what your adaptation tune-up will require.
4. Decide if it's worth it.

Drive Carefully: Don't Skid on Corporate Politics

Janice: Particularly today, how do you recommend avoiding political corporations?

Bill: It's a way of life: you have to be politically astute and understand the politics. If you don't, you can get caught in a crossfire of bullets. It is messy, but it is also what makes it possible to get things done.

Janice: So the politics make for a slippery road ahead.

Bill: No doubt about it.

Janice: Let's look at how to drive on a slippery road and still get to our destination—safely!

Bill: You have such a way with words . . .

A POLITICS-FREE ORGANIZATION?

Fresh out of business school and burning with the desire to do well in corporate life, Joe vowed he would eschew politics—which he defined as keeping an eye always on the main chance and scratching another's back so he could get his scratched in turn—and "simply do the job." He would play by the rules, carry out his assignments, remain civil and friendly and cooperative, and succeed on merit and performance—nothing else. That was the pledge he made, and as he showed up for work on Day One, the mantra he kept repeating to himself was this: *No politics, no hassles. No politics, no hassles. No politics, no hassles.*

Good luck, Joe.

In a way, of course, Joe has it right. If there were no politics, there might well be fewer hassles in corporate life. But we are here to tell you that there is no such thing as an organization without politics. Never has been, never will be. So Joe's mantra of no politics, no hassles, simply is not going to happen. Politics is as intrinsic to corporate life as the profit motive or the setting of goals or the corporate Christmas party where at least one person makes a fool of himself.

What's more, you find politics everywhere—not just in corporations but in schools, hospitals, nonprofit foundations, among athletes and booksellers, in families, in the military, on the seas, and almost surely in outer space, not to mention at every level of government from the local planning board to the U.S. Supreme Court. You simply can't avoid politics.

Nor should you.

In Washington, just about anything is fodder for one party to complain loudly that the other party is "playing politics" with an issue. Well, of course they are. Both parties are playing politics all the time. Politics, after all, is the game, and there's a good reason why.

Nobody said it better than President John F. Kennedy back in 1960, when he was candidate Kennedy. "Senator," he was asked, "why do you want to be president of the United States?"

Kennedy didn't hesitate. "Because that's where the power is," he said bluntly.

That's what it comes down to: power—the power to get things

done. Having the power to get things done and, it is hoped, using the power wisely and well are essential to going forward on the career highway. Sometimes, to be sure, politics can make the road very slippery indeed. Such situations will require special handling as you steer into the skid in order to right your wheels. But politics can also be the way you extricate yourself from such a situation. It isn't a dirty word. It's a fact of life that can work for you or against you—depending on how well you play it. It isn't just that you can't avoid politics; it's that you can't afford to neglect it.

> Politics is the art of the possible.
>
> —OTTO VON BISMARCK, CHANCELLOR OF GERMANY, 1815–1898

So here are three key tasks to help you navigate the slippery and sometimes dangerous road of politics. At the least, performing these tasks will keep you from overturning. More likely, they'll help you get where you're going. At best, they may help you drive right to the top.

TASK 1: CARPOOL WITH ALLIES YOU CAN COUNT ON (WHO'S IN THE CAR WITH YOU?)

In politics, alliances are crucial, and in a corporation, peer support is just as important as the boss's approval. In fact, some political analysts believe it is more important. After all, you can gain your boss's go-ahead on a project, but if you don't have peer support for it, your efforts can be gradually eroded to nothing. Peers don't actually have to be *against* you; they need only be *not for* you to have a braking effect on your forward motion.

Five political allies or supporters among your peers is an ideal number, but numbers aren't the whole story. At least some of the five need to wield power or influence—or both—in the organization. One might have the ear of a top-level manager. Another might be a well-positioned staff person, who always knows who's up and who's down. Yet another might be an obvious star, someone being groomed for promotion at any moment. The point is this: if people of this caliber support you, others will hear about it, for while all support is good, the support of the powerful is better. It goes further, and it works harder.

That's why it's essential to analyze where your support is, how valuable it is, and how reliable it is.

Start by asking yourself who in the organization supports you. Who among your peers is an ally? Are these allies public about their support? What does their support consist of—good wishes or demonstrable actions? To what extent do you trust them—how much can you rely on them? And how influential are they in the organization—what buttons can they push, and what will be the impact?

Answer these questions in the following chart, and you will have a good idea of which passengers are riding with you to your goal, and which are just along for show.

PASSENGERS IN MY CAR

Peers Who Openly Support Me	How They Support Me	How Much I Trust Them (1 low/5 high)	How Influential They Are (1 low/5 high)
1.			
2.			
3.			
4.			
5.			

Remember the number five; that's the number of influential and knowledgeable supporters you'd like to have helping you navigate the slippery road of corporate power. And also remember that you cannot do it alone. So assess who your supporters are—and cherish them.

One way to do that is to support them in turn. Political support is a two-way street, after all, and just as it's important to have supporters among your peers, it's equally important to be one *for* your peers. As always, it's best to be a supporter of people with power and influence in the organization—for two reasons. First, it is good to be associated with rising stars. Second, when those stars reciprocate the support, it will make a louder noise and increase your visibility and stature in the organization.

Fill out the following chart about the people you carpool with. How have you demonstrated your support of these people recently? How can you demonstrate your support in the future? Which of them are more influential or powerful in the organization?

THE PEERS I RIDE WITH

Peers I Support	How I Have Demonstrated My Support	How I Can Demonstrate Support in Future	Who Is Most Influential in the Organization (1 low/5 high)
1.			
2.			
3.			
4.			
5.			

Finally, while it's good to know that there is a carload of people who are political allies, it's essential to know who among your peers *cannot* be counted as a supporter. The chart below will help you ascertain who's throwing eggs at your car. List the people you know are against you—that is, the people you cannot count on for support. Why don't they support you? Is it because they perceive you as a rival with similar ambitions, or is it because they perceive that your goals are so different from theirs that you must always be at loggerheads? Whatever the reason, how does this lack of support play out? Here are some questions to determine the type of "adversary" you face:

- Do these nonsupporters deliberately want you to fail, and are they acting overtly to thwart your success?
- Are they trying to hog more credit for themselves but not deliberately trying to hurt you?
- Are they just oblivious and concentrating on being a steamroller?

Can you win any of these nonsupporters to your side? How? How can you convince them that their self-interest is closely bound up with yours? Failing that, how can you keep out of their way— and keep them out of your way?

WHO'S THROWING EGGS AT MY CAR?

Nonsupporting Peers	Why? Which of the Above Three Are They?	How to Win Them Over or Avoid Them
1.		
2.		
3.		

Nonsupporting Peers	Why? Which of the Above Three Are They?	How to Win Them Over or Avoid Them
4.		
5.		

Take a close look at the three charts you have just completed to see who and what constitute your car pool—your political support—and where you cannot find support. Ask yourself these questions:

- Are your supporters reliable but not influential?
- Who are your influential and realistic supporters?
- Are the people in your car pool grateful for your support?
- Do the egg throwers actively work against you and hurt you, or just ignore you because they are self-absorbed?

The answers will serve as a profile of where your car pool needs shoring up—additional members? replacement members?—and where you run the risk of colliding with those ready to throw eggs. With that information, you can work to redress the imbalances and fill your car with supporters so strong and influential that the egg throwers will just stay home.

Task 2: Cultivate the Company Stars

"Hitch your wagon to a star," the old saying goes, and there's a good reason for it. You shine in the star's light, and the brightness radiates outward—particularly if and when you have been responsible for helping make the star shine. In other words, make someone look good, and you look good too.

The lesson is obvious. Identify the stars in your organization, cultivate them, and help them shine. And be assured of this: anyone who has become a star in the organization knows how its politics work. You help their agenda, and they're bound to help yours. Over time, as you support their causes, projects, and efforts—providing of course that you believe in them too—they increasingly see you as a supportive passenger in their car, and they will be ready to ride in your car as well.

The first thing to do, therefore, is to identify the company stars. Usually, they light up all by themselves. You rarely have to go searching for them; you can spot them from miles away. They're the ones who get the promotions, get the press coverage, and get talked about. It's worth studying these people to learn what it is about them that the company values—and to think about how you might learn to shine in the same way.

Here's a chart to help you log the company stars. Note the person's name and title; then jot down his or her most recent notable action or achievement. What's the last thing the person did or said or achieved that made people sit up and take notice—and perhaps got them to start using the word *star* to describe the person? Now dig deeper to analyze just what it is that makes this person a star at this company—i.e., what value does the company place on this person? Finally, it's important to note who in the company values the person. Does he or she have a powerful mentor or supporter advancing his or her interests? If so, that may be someone you need to cultivate as well.

DRIVING WITH THE STARS

Name	Title	Most Recent Notable Action or Achievement	Value in the Company's Eye	Who in the Company Values the Person?

The actual work of cultivating comes next. You cultivate company stars the same way you cultivate plants: find out what makes them thrive, and feed it to them. Most stars rise as their agendas succeed, so nurture their agendas—and let them see you doing it. It's fine to voice your support loud enough for the stars to hear about it; so long as you don't sound like a sycophant, it will gain you mileage. Help the stars sell their ideas or achieve their targeted objectives. Run interference for them if they exhibit a political blind spot, and serve on defense against political predators who may want to tackle or undermine your chosen stars. Help them advance both their business priorities and their political aims, for each serves the other, and as you serve both, you'll gain some of that reflected glory.

TASK 3: FOR YOUR OWN ADVANCEMENT, SPEND 20 PERCENT OF YOUR TIME TAKING CARE OF THE POLITICS OF YOUR CAREER

It's easy to get caught up doing what you're comfortable doing. But if you are going to avoid delays on the career highway, you absolutely have to pay attention to the politics in the organization. That's why we've devised our version of the 80–20 rule. It's pretty simple: spend 80 percent of your time doing the job you're being paid to do, and spend 20 percent of your time advancing your career by marketing yourself to others who will be your influential supporters.

"Hold on!" we hear you saying. "I can barely do the job I'm paid to do with 100 percent of my time. The job is simply too big to take time away from it." Oh, really? Just how big *is* your job? For each major task for which you are responsible, ask yourself these questions:

1. Is it visible to the organization's leadership?
2. Does it have an impact beyond your department?

3. Is it strategic to the organization's goals?
4. If you fail at it, will it cause significant disruption in the corporation or impact the company's reputation?
5. Does it hit the bottom line—directly?

If you answered *no* to three out of these five questions, then your responsibilities aren't so weighty that you can't delegate those tasks to others if you are in a position to do so, or negotiate your way out of them if you are not in a position to do so. Either way, always make sure that you follow up. In other words, the parts of your job that are not valued by the company constitute work you don't have to do yourself. On the contrary, it's work you should not do. It is a fuel leak—insignificant to your higher purpose, and it should simply be delegated. Ditto for the people who take up a lot of your time and only succeed in letting air out of your tires. Dump them as well. Time cannot be replaced, but you can be if you don't use your time wisely.

By downloading the work that is insignificant in terms of what the company values, and by shifting the personnel who simply suck the oxygen out of the room, we're certain you'll free up at least 20 percent of your time for that other big task and responsibility: advancing your career.

The time is now! Figure out where your fuel leak is and how you can assign someone else to find the resources to stanch the flow. Here's the exercise that will help you assess whether each element of your work responsibility can be delegated elsewhere:

On the chart below, first describe your key tasks or responsibilities. Check off whether each is *visible, has wide impact,* is of *strategic importance* to the organization, could cause organizational *disruption* or impact the company's *reputation* if it is done badly or late or not at all, and affects the *bottom line.*

FINDING THE FUEL LEAK

Effects / Describe Your *Key Tasks*	Visible?	Of Wide Impact?	Strategic?	Something That Causes Disruption/ Impacts Reputation?	Something That Affects Bottom Line?
Task 1 Time to do the work: ____					
Task 2 Time to do the work: ____					
Task 3 Time to do the work: ____					

Total it up. Then assess your data. If a task has none of the effects noted but takes up four days a month, it's time to turn that responsibility over to the others on the team. If a task has all of the effects noted, it's yours to carry out; wherever your absence from

> Man is by nature a
> political animal.
>
> —ARISTOTLE,
> 384–322 BC

a task would have costly ramifications, you need to be there. Such situations require your full and complete attention and involvement, because mistakes made on tasks of this importance can be fatal; it's hard to undo the harm to your reputation. Mistakes will occur, of course, but make sure they occur only in the low-impact, low-visibility, low-importance tasks; that's like getting a flat tire: fix it and drive on.

Our bet is that a goodly number of the work steps you identify have little or no impact in terms of what your organization values. Let someone else do them while you concentrate on the work that counts, that gets recognized, and that can move you forward on your career highway.

SUMMARY

Politics is a fact of corporate life, which you neglect at your peril. Instead, play politics in such a way that everyone wins, especially you. Here's how:

1. Carpool with allies you can count on. (Who's in the car with you?)
2. Cultivate the company stars.
3. For your own political advancement, follow the 80–20 rule. Dump insignificant tasks and the people who just let air of your tires.

Bosses Matter: Learn How
to Manage Your Boss

Bill: There are bosses and then there are *bosses.* The trick is getting one who will not only help you navigate your career highway but will also help you get to your destination without accidents or delays.

Janice: Yes, and many of the people I interview for jobs really are running away—mainly from their boss—not usually the company. Being put in charge of people is a competency a lot of bosses do not do well, if at all.

Bill: That's a clear road sign for every professional: you must get through that dark tunnel of managing your boss so that you don't get run off the road. And if you can't manage the boss, you may have to find another road.

Janice: And reading the signals that you are getting from your boss correctly will help to make the ride an easier and more productive one for your career.

THE X FACTOR ON YOUR CAREER HIGHWAY

On the train to work Friday morning, Caroline went over her mental checklist in preparation for the big presentation to the CFO. The slides were set—beautifully prepared by Graphics—and had been programmed onto her laptop. The projection screen was already in the conference room. She had carefully planned what she would wear, she already knew what she'd have for breakfast before the presentation, and she more than knew what she was going to say. She had her facts down pat, she had structured the presentation as an almost dramatic narrative—with a rising arc of suspense—and she knew the "ask" she was going to end with. She even thought she knew how the CFO would respond, and she was ready for him.

The only question mark in the whole thing, in fact, was her boss. Although she had tried to *suggest* to Ned how he might position the presentation, the guy was a wild card: unpredictable, unreadable, and utterly unmanageable. She was never sure where she was with him, and she was never sure what he wanted, what he was saying, or what he might do. The guy was a dark tunnel she could never see into, and the danger was that he would go off on some tangent, as he frequently did, and ramble, leaving her out of the picture and turning her into little more than a footnote as far as the CFO was concerned. This made him the X factor not just of her job, but of her career management task—an unknown quantity she did not control. Ned was basically a good guy—very sharp, very conscientious—but he undermanaged, when he managed at all, and that made her work life not just difficult but sometimes, like this morning, downright dangerous . . .

Managing up. There's nothing tougher. Managing subordinates is a piece of cake by comparison. For one thing, when you manage down, you start off with the power of review and the power of the purse, and so you begin from a position of authority. Having some measure of say-so over people's jobs, compensation packages, and lives—while a formidable responsibility—actually provides a structure within which you can provide direction and exert control.

Not so with your boss, of course. It takes a whole different set of skills and techniques to manage a superior, but it is essential for keeping your car tooling fast and straight down the career highway.

For one thing, some bosses are just not very good at being the boss. A lot of bosses overmanage. You're given an assignment and told to execute it—and there's the boss, hanging over your shoulder every second, monitoring the project's status. Others undermanage, and, like Caroline, you find yourself adrift with insufficient direction, inadequate feedback, and not enough resources for doing the job. And some bosses are just inept: fearful of losing their jobs, power hungry, moody, just plain mean, or—perhaps worst of all—absent. Whatever the situation, an inadequate boss can suck all the creativity out of your work life, dampen your enthusiasm, even curb your productivity. In short, a bad boss can create an employee who cannot win, much less survive the career highway: reason one why you need to manage up.

GETTING IT RIGHT FROM THE START: EVALUATE YOUR BOSS WHEN INTERVIEWING HIM OR HER

One way to be sure you're working for a good boss you can manage well is to choose the boss yourself before you take the job. Next time you go for a job interview, whether it's an internal lateral move or a jump to a new company, watch for these key warning signs; they'll tell you a lot about the person you may be working for. Note (Y/N) after the interview whether your potential boss did any of the following:

1. ____ Arrived late for the interview—even though it had already been postponed at least once.
2. ____ Couldn't find your résumé.
3. ____ Frequently interrupted the conversation to take calls, check e-mails, or glance at the time. Clearly neither you—nor the position you're interviewing for—is this person's highest priority.
4. ____ Talked about his/her accomplishments without giving others credit—i.e., is afflicted by the "I" Syndrome
5. ____ Appeared frazzled and barked at the administrative assistant or another staffer.
6. ____ Stirred no chemistry between the two of you.
7. ____ With a limp handshake, arms crossed, and a refusal to make eye contact across a desk divider that looked like a medieval fortress, signaled that your relationship would not be a collaborative one.

If your interview produced three "Yes" designations, think hard about working for this individual. If it produced five or more, you might do well to walk away now.

Trust your gut about the interview, but also get confirmation from people who have left the company—and share your feelings with a coach or with a trusted friend.

If this potential boss is clearly not someone you would want to work for, prepare a list of the

> Accomplishing the impossible means only that the boss will add it to your regular duties.
>
> —DOUG LARSON, AMERICAN BUSINESSMAN

traits that bother you about the person; then set down the ideal traits you would want in your next boss—and keep this in mind at your next interview.

Here are some classic bad-boss traits: narcissistic, paranoid, controlling, inept, unconsciously incompetent, consciously incompetent, a bully, a glory seeker, takes all the credit and gives little, not available, not approachable, extremely/unfairly political, leaves people twisting in the wind, moody, unpredictable, dictatorial, absent, not respected, bad communicator.

DO YOU HAVE A "BAD" BOSS?

We wrote "bad" in quotes because we don't mean a bad person; we just mean a boss who undermanages, overmanages, or perhaps simply fails to manage at all—and who leaves you less enthusiastic and less productive than you might be about your work. By taking a close look at the bad-boss indicators lighting up on your dashboard, you'll be drawing a picture of the kind of boss you'd like to have next—and perhaps also of the kind of boss you ought to be.

The bad-boss indicator lights are specific behaviors that start flashing when you see your own performance and future fading out because you can't deal with the boss. Write those behaviors down here, and then set down the ideal behavior that would quickly turn off the bad-boss indicator light and help you do your job better.

Boss's Behavior That Turns On the Bad-Boss Indicator Light	Ideal Behavior That Would Turn Off the Bad-Boss Indicator Light

But the truth is that even the best boss in the world needs to be managed. Whether you were personally chosen by your boss or you "inherited" him or her, your wagon is inevitably hitched to the boss's star. You're *associated with* the boss, and his or her performance, reputation, abilities, and image in the company invariably reflect on you—often to the point where the way you're perceived is conflated with the way the boss is perceived.

Yet the most important reason you need to manage your boss, good or bad, is this: there's no person more important to your career at any one moment than your boss. It's your boss who handed you the keys to the car, and it's your boss who can take the keys away, get a duplicate set made for someone else, toss them out the window and make you scramble for them, or hand you a new set of keys to a bigger, shinier car. Moreover, unless the boss is riding shotgun with you on your career highway, supporting you every mile of the way, the road beneath your wheels can become dangerously slick. No one else in the organization has as direct an impact on your career progress or on the direction in which it goes. So learning to manage the boss must be part of your professional education.

TASK 1: PROFILE THE BOSS (WHO *IS* THIS PERSON YOU WORK FOR?)

If you're going to manage the boss, you first need to know who he or she is. Use the following chart to paint a portrait of the individual you report to. You'll have to do some incisive thinking in this exercise, and you'll need to rely on a sixth sense to pick up on the unspoken signals every individual sends out. In this case, those signals will likely concern those things your boss cannot or will not let you in on because of comfort level, fear of litigation, or the sense that you will pick up on it in any event.

Basically, what you're trying to articulate are the qualities, talents, and personal and political connections your boss brings to his or her job and place in the organization—and the weaknesses, failures, and areas of incompetence or indifference he or she exhibits. For example, Bill tells of a guy he coached—we'll call him Pete—who was merely competent at the main task assigned to him, but who had such a forceful and charismatic personality that others around the organization simply deferred to him. Yet another interesting boss—we'll call her Nancy—was an absolute whiz at what she did in managing a large division, yet neither the job nor managing interested her; all she cared about was the politics of the place. Not surprisingly, Nancy was a lot easier to manage up than Pete was.

Note your boss's strengths and weaknesses. Where is he or she "merely competent" like Pete, and to what is your boss indifferent, as Nancy was? What does the boss find easy to do—and what gives him or her problems?

Now put yourself inside your boss's head and heart and try to determine, from all you sense about this person, exactly what he or she aspires to. In dealing with people at any level on any subject, it's usually possible to tell after a while what their true ambition or ultimate goal is. Try to ascertain your boss's hoped-for aim. Write it down. It should tell you a lot about this person you report to.

BOSS PROFILE

Boss's Strengths	Boss's Weaknesses	Boss's Aspirations—Where S/he Wants to Go

TASK 2: PROFILE YOUR RELATIONSHIP WITH THE BOSS

Once you know who your boss really is, you need to look at your relationship with your boss.

First, what does your boss expect of you? Use the chart below to list at least three expectations your boss has "told" you are foremost in his or her mind—and should therefore be foremost in *your* mind.

Second, what do you believe are your boss's unspoken expectations of you? Again, set down three things you think the boss wants from you—perhaps concerning the way you dress, or a commitment of time in the office, or certain proficiencies you bring to the job.

THE BOSS'S EXPECTATIONS

Spoken Expectations	Unspoken Expectations

Third, what is the bottom-line appraisal of you that you have heard from your boss? Write down the three top words you know your boss would use to describe you.

WHAT THE BOSS SAYS ABOUT ME

1. _____

2. _____

3. _____

Finally, write down three words your boss has not used that you think really describe what he or she thinks of you.

WHAT I THINK THE BOSS REALLY THINKS OF ME

1. _____

2. _____

3. _____

Knowing your relationship with your boss is your reality check before taking action to manage the boss.

TASK 3: MAKE YOUR RELATIONSHIP WITH THE BOSS WORK TO ACHIEVE HIS/HER ASPIRATIONS—THAT IS, MANAGE UP!

Now that you know who your boss is and where and how you believe you stand in relation to him or her, it's time to figure out how to influence, manipulate, direct—if possible—and simply *handle* the boss. In short, it's time to plan how to manage up.

There's a simple way to carry out this task. Go back to the Boss Profile you created in Task 1, and add a fourth column to the chart in which you determine how you can enhance the boss's strengths and shore up the boss's weaknesses to advance him or her toward the aspirations you've articulated.

Boss's Strengths	Boss's Weaknesses	Boss's Aspirations	How Can I Enhance Boss's Strengths and Shore Up Weaknesses to Help Achieve Boss's Aspirations?

The reality check of understanding the boss's true perception of you is essential to the management task. You cannot really change your boss, but you can change how he or she perceives you. If you believe the boss secretly thinks you're lazy, you will need to change that perception if you want to manage the boss toward taking bold action. If you believe the boss thinks you have no interest but self-interest, you must show him or her that his or her self-interest is what matters. If you suspect the boss finds you loyal, steadfast, and true, you must also show the boss you see things through his or her eyes—and will use your loyalty to help.

WILL FLATTERY GET YOU SOMEWHERE
WHEN YOU'RE MANAGING THE BOSS?

Studies say the answer is a qualified yes—to both flattering the boss and cozying up to him or her with friendly "schmoozing." A University of Michigan psychologist, Randall Gordon, collected data from nearly 70 studies on the issue and concluded that "ingratiation shrewdly employed will get you ahead. If you have two people who are both competent at what they do, but one is really good at schmoozing . . . the one likely to get the raise is the schmoozer. It gives you the edge."

In addition, a review of 152 sets of supervisors and employees, all of whom conceded that they tried to flatter their bosses, revealed that the flatterers scored 5 percent higher in their performance evaluations than the non-flatterers. According to the study's author, Ronald Deluga of Bryant College, "No one wants to do it [flatter the boss], but you are at a disadvantage if you don't—and no one wants to take that risk."

Basically, what you're doing when you try to manage up is looking at things from the boss's perspective, trying to understand the boss's problem, and making the boss's ambitions your own. Nothing is better calculated or better suited to managing the boss—or anyone else—than supporting that person in achieving his or her dreams. By consciously working with your boss to obtain the best possible results he or she can achieve, you invariably obtain better results for yourself.

Does this mean you give up your own ambitions in favor of the boss's? Absolutely not. It means that you use the boss's ambitions—and your help in achieving them—as an on-ramp to your own career highway.

Does it mean you become a yes-man to everything the boss says or suggests or demands? Again, absolutely not! What it means is that when your boss says no to your killer idea, you write her a memo showing how the idea can advance what you now understand to be her goals—and you make it clear, without actually saying so, that the killer idea will also show off her strengths and, off the record, cover up her weaknesses. It means that when the boss breaks a commitment to you, you complain in terms of how the broken commitment diminishes your ability to help the boss advance toward his aspiration. Again, you don't say this in so many words, but keep the boss's viewpoint in mind. Your purpose, in short, is to help the boss achieve his or her purpose. Keep that purpose in mind, and you'll become an expert in managing up.

SUMMARY

It's the boss who can pull you over, stall your engine, or actually stop your forward progress on the career highway. To keep your boss riding shotgun with you all the way, you have to learn to manage the boss. Here's how:

1. Profile the boss. (Who *is* this person you work for?)
2. Profile your relationship with the boss.
3. Make your relationship with the boss work to achieve his/her aspirations—that is, manage up!

Avoid Being Crushed: Learn to Manage the People Around You

Bill: What do you do when the people you work with seem to be turning against you—when they cross the solid double line to pass and come into your lane? They are speeding along without concern for others in their way even though they are in your space—your lane!

Janice: My clients tell me that, yes, they want to recruit rainmakers, but they also want them to be team players—not stars who hog the road and try to get all the credit.

Bill: Being an individual and a team contributor is a balancing act. You don't want it to look like your show. You need to give others credit.

Janice: Absolutely. People need to know you support them, will give them credit—that they can trust you.

Bill: It all comes down to the fact that everyone needs his or her own raving fan club. People are much quicker to support you if they like you and respect you.

PEOPLE POWER

George was thrilled when he received his long-sought promotion and the chance at long last to manage a department. He was determined to succeed in his new position, and he fully expected that the very attributes that had gotten him this far would take him to the success he wanted: clarity of purpose, absolute precision in planning, intolerance of deviation from plan, and what he liked to call "execution on a war footing." He began with enthusiasm, calling a meeting of the entire department and announcing, in a slightly stilted speech (George was a clear communicator, but not an easy one) exactly what he expected from "the troops."

> A sense of humor is part of the art of leadership, of getting along with people, of getting things done.
>
> —Dwight D. Eisenhower, 1890–1969

And then he proceeded to fail miserably, but not because the purpose wasn't clear or the plan precise. Quite the opposite: there wasn't a person in the department who couldn't recite every objective and tick off the plan details with mathematical exactitude. On the other hand, no one in the department much cared whether George's plan succeeded or not, so when it became advisable to deviate from the plan just a bit, and when George vetoed the very thought of deviating, people just shrugged and did as they were told. Bottom line? Execution certainly was on a war footing, but the war, as it turned out, was between George and the people who worked for him. And the result was failure.

The lesson? Your career, like your life, is with people. You can have all the savvy in the world, all the determination you can muster, all the militarylike engineering precision you want, but you still need the hearts and minds of the people you work with if you're going to drive the career highway without accident or emergency stopping toward your goal.

Here's a visualization game: Close your eyes and imagine a bird's-eye view of your company. Think of it not as the location you go to every day to earn a living but as a community of people. There they all are, going about their business with varying levels of energy and enthusiasm. Way up in the vast corner office sits the chairman, surrounded by aides, cosseted by deputies, nurtured by assistants, and trying hard not to be isolated. Floor by floor, in smaller corner offices, are the corporation's equivalent of a community's infrastructure: the hierarchy of officers with a stake in the company's performance and future, the people who manage the business and hold it together and worry about how well they're doing both activities. Finally, bustling about from floor to floor, there is the vast pool of functionaries who execute the day-to-day operations of the company, plus all the support staff—everything from secretaries to input clerks to drivers to messengers and custodians.

There are two facts about the people breezing along in this hub of activity that are particularly pertinent to your career. Fact number one is that not everybody you see in this visualization can be of assistance in your career, although some people certainly can be. As mentors, as friends, or out of a self-interest that your advancement also serves, people will reach out to help you steer in the right direction or at the right speed or on the right road to your career goals. Such people are to be cherished and thanked, and their help is to be reciprocated whenever and however possible.

Fact number two is that just about anybody in the place can puncture your tire—superiors to be sure, but also subordinates, support staff, and your coworkers and coequals: your peers. If and when that happens, you'll have all you can do to retain control and avoid being rammed off the highway.

And here's an addendum to both facts: there is nothing static about the cast of characters willing and able to help or hurt your career. Some of those you think would help your career will move on, move out, or turn out to be ineffectual. Meanwhile, the new hire who shyly asked you this morning if she could work on your marketing presentation will leap tall buildings in a single bound, and you'll find yourself reporting to her next year—when she'll fondly remember how welcoming and helpful you were. At the same time, the coworker you thought was a real pal—enough of a pal that you could confide your real feelings about the boss to him—will turn out to be a conniving manipulator to whom friendship means nothing and for whom every bit of information is a weapon to be held in reserve until it's time to fire it off. Let's face it, corporate life is a minefield.

> If you don't know what to do with many of the papers piled on your desk, stick a dozen colleagues' initials on 'em, and pass them along. When in doubt, route.
>
> —MALCOLM FORBES, AMERICAN PUBLISHER, 1919–1990

Are we saying that the bottom line here is "Be nice"? You bet we are. Treat everyone with respect and friendliness. It's smart, it's safe, and it's the right thing to do. You never know who could end up being your fairy godmother and who could stab you in the back later on.

But there is more to it than that. Everyone else in your workplace drives a car on the career highway too. You don't want to be surprised to find that they're all going in another direction from you, and that they're going so fast and so hard that rocks are beginning to fall onto the highway—your highway, not theirs.

PEERS, FANS, AND MAKING
THE FORMER THE LATTER

You need peers in your career. You need them to stage battles with you and to help you win wars. Nobody succeeds alone in corporate America. The pace of business and the dominance of technology make that simply impossible. Numerous skills and resources are needed to make anything happen, which is why all those HR officers tell Janice and other executive recruiters that they will not consider anyone with a reputation as "an accident waiting to happen," a loner, or a do-it-yourselfer. They want team members; in fact, they want likeable team members.

Being nice, however, simply isn't sufficient. Instead, you need to be proactive on two fronts. First, you must create what we like to refer to as "raving fans"—giving credit to Ken Blanchard and Sheldon Bowles, who wrote the book[1] on the subject. Raving fans are the people within the corporation who respect you and who see their own self-interest inextricably tied up with furthering yours. It's a universal reality: people are much more apt to help and/or follow someone they like and respect.

Second, you must manage your fellow workers. For here's another universal reality: people tend to respond better to team members than to the officials in charge; in fact, the latter are often perceived as the common enemy. It's why army grunts often don't like officers, why newspaper reporters resent newspaper publishers, why the rank-and-filers fight the big boss they don't know and never even see.

The reason is simple: team relationships engender trust. People who work together come to depend on one another; they face the same day-to-day challenges, speak the same language, inhabit the same world. They understand one another and the job they do together, and they feel—rightly, much of the time—that those who have power over them don't share in that understanding. Managing your peers means making sure they see you as a team member, so that when you need them to be a "sales force" for your career, they'll be there.

So here is a three-task process for making sure you will have the people power you need when you need it.

TASK 1: FIND OUT HOW YOU'RE PERCEIVED

Want to know how well liked you are—that is, how much support you can count on if and when you need it? Ask. Not formally and not outright, but gradually and comprehensively.

Start by creating your own personal 360 list. Look around you—all around you, the full 360 degrees—and list the subordinates, coequals, supervisors, and others with whom you interact regularly, frequently, even just occasionally. Write it down.

	Interact Very Often	Interact Frequently	Interact Occasionally
Subordinates Name			
Name			
Name			
Coequals Name			
Name			
Name			
Supervisors Name			

	Interact Very Often	Interact Frequently	Interact Occasionally
Name			
Name			
Externals Name			
Name			
Name			

Now fold the list into a six-month schedule of lunches, coffee breaks, or other forms of informal meetings. Make sure you meet with each person on your list at least twice during the six months. At each meeting, ask for feedback on your performance in general and on your interaction with the individual in particular. At the end of each meeting, assure the person that you would welcome ongoing feedback and request each of them to advise you on how you are doing. Everyone likes to advise, right?

The six-month effort should show you clearly how you're perceived by those you work with and should serve as a guide directing you toward actions you should take. Where you sense you're not well regarded, get to work becoming more accepted and respected. Where you see that you are well thought of, strengthen that base even more with further effort.

Task 2: Make an Effort to Gain Affection as Well as Support

How does one become better liked? Obviously, we are not here to bend your personality out of its natural shape into another. But in a work situation, there are some things an individual can do that cut across all levels of the hierarchy—subordinates, coequals, and supervisors—to leave an impression of both affability and competence, the kind of impression that makes people want to work with you and for you. Here are our top three tips for becoming more likeable—and better liked:

Tip 1: Be supportive.

There are few things more attractive to people than having you support them in their efforts. Obviously, this doesn't mean you should accede to every request or rubber-stamp every proposal. It does mean you should approach every request and proposal with sensitivity and openness; look for a way to say, "Yes, you have my support [or approval]"—if not to everything, then to some part of what is being put before you. Try to remove "Yes, but . . ." from your vocabulary; it's shorthand for "No," and it's a downer. Above all, don't whine, complain, or commiserate with whiners and complainers. That just saps energy and plunges everyone into negative territory. Do the opposite: make it a goal to energize people in every meeting and interaction in which you participate—not out of blind cheerfulness, like some Pollyanna, but because it's a way of getting people to work together toward a common goal.

Tip 2: Do the little things.

Sally picked up the phone in her office and heard, through the din at the other end of the line, the voice of her boss, Ed, calling from the conference in Seattle. "Sally?" he said over the ambient cacophony. "I just came out of the meeting hall, and I wanted to tell you that the presentation went wonderfully. You did a great job, and I can't thank you enough. It's a real winner."

Sally felt herself blushing with pride and pleasure. "Thank you, Ed. Thank you for calling."

"Thank *you*, Sally."

Sally swiveled in her chair, still beaming, only to confront her highly cynical office mate, Alan. "It's a ploy," Alan commented after Sally told him about Ed's call. "They learn it in that charm school all top managers have to go to: 'Don't forget to be nice to the peons.' Calling to thank you was just a gimmick, Sal."

"It may be a gimmick," Sally replied. "But it's working."

That's the thing about so-called "small" gestures like Ed's phone call: they work. In the office, as anywhere else, courtesies, compliments, making an effort to praise someone, going out of your way to be helpful, all of these things make people feel good, and people who feel good about you are people prepared to support your endeavors and follow where you career highway leads.

Tip 3: Demonstrate an ability to change.

This is a hard one. Remember all that feedback you were searching out from the people on your 360 list in Task 1? In Task 2, you need to show that you heard the feedback and are doing something about it. No, it isn't easy to admit your own shortcomings, but let's face it: when it comes to professional development as well as life as a whole, absolutely no one is perfect. We can all use improvement. Demonstrating that you value the feedback of others and are capable of making the changes they've suggested shows a personal strength that is worthy of their respect and warrants their support.

Task 3: Proactively Manage Your Peers

While you are working on gaining general support on a comprehensive, 360-degree scale, you must simultaneously concentrate on peer management through a more tightly focused lens. You are looking here for the key players who can constitute your personal "sales force"—that core of peers you can count on to share your objectives and work with you to achieve them. At the same time, you want to locate those peers you definitely cannot count on—not to mention those who might actually cause a career accident.

Step One is to identify both sets of peers, both the potential sales force and the possible troublemakers. For your sales force, you are looking for people who can cover the entire life cycle of the "product," which in this case is, simply and quite baldly, your advancement along the career highway. Start by listing five key peers; the hope is that you will add to the sales force over time. To find the five, ask yourself who in the organization you would go to, before you go to a supervisor, should an issue arise or a problem surface. Set down what each of the five does and his or her relationship to you—that is, the capacities in which you work with the person—as follows:

MY PERSONAL SALES FORCE

Name	Function	Relationship

Unhappily, you need to do the same thing for prospective troublemakers—those people who could conceivably impede your forward progress or actually harm your career. To find them, think back on your career thus far: Who has put up obstacles to you in the past? Who is a rival for the same wedge of pie for which you hunger? Where are these people in the organization, and what levers of power do they hold? Go back to Chapter 7 and look at the chart showing the egg throwers. Clearly, the presence of more than three potential troublemakers in key positions is a major red flag on your career highway.

MY POTENTIAL TROUBLEMAKERS

Name	Function	Hierarchical Level/ Levers of Power

Task 3 should now be clear. For those peers who constitute your potential personal sales team, determine what you can do to help each of them help you.

MY PERSONAL SALES TEAM

Name	Function	Relationship	Helping Action

For those peers who might conceivably put roadblocks in your way or actually try to run you off the road, what steps can you take to change their perceptions, neutralize them, or at least contain them?

MY POTENTIAL TROUBLEMAKERS

Name	Function	Hierarchical Level/Levers of Power	Change	Neutralize	Contain

Certainly, it is not pleasant to think about people who may not wish you well, or to devise strategies for counteracting their possibly harmful actions. And cooking up tactics for helping supporters can also sound manipulative and disingenuous. But in today's corporate environment, which is and will remain determinedly team oriented, it would be foolish to ignore or dismiss these realities of corporate life. And it would be downright negligent not to prepare yourself to deal with their impact on your ride down the career highway.

SUMMARY

Obviously, the people you work with can be either a help or a hindrance to your career. To make sure they're in your lane and not bearing down on you as oncoming traffic, do the following:

1. Find out how you're perceived.
2. Make an effort to gain affection as well as support.
3. Proactively manage your peers: help your potential sales team; change your prospective troublemakers.

Get in the Fast Lane: Learn How to Compete So You Win

Bill: We're constantly being told that an organization is a competitive arena and that we have to fight to get ahead. What about today's job candidates? Are they fighters?

Janice: Some shy away from the battle; others are so combative they're not well received. The most talented are not afraid of competition but do it in a winning way. They understand it's how you compete that counts.

Bill: Competition is healthy, and there's competition in everything. When we wake up every day, we're competing for resources, money, status, prestige, good friends. All of this really advances humanity.

Janice: Sure. Being competitive is good for the organization. The organization exists to win, and the people in the organization are there to make that happen.

Bill: In a global context, it's a win-win situation if all people and countries compete so that others can also be strong. That improves the power of trade and of global economic well-being.

Janice: For now, let's focus on the power of one.

COMPETING TO WIN

Everybody competes. But not everybody wins. That's the daily reality in any organization.

At the start of a career, you and all your colleagues are on a superhighway with multiple lanes. It's wide enough for all of you to ride along together, without getting in one another's way, without having to resort to lane changes and fancy maneuvering to get where you're going. But as you advance upward on the highway, the road narrows. The reason is simple: there are far fewer positions available in the upper reaches of the hierarchy, so there are more of you vying for the positions than there are positions to go around. Yet the top is where many want to be, and if you have the same vision, it is what you have been training for and working toward. So as the road narrows, all those coworkers and you get squeezed into ever tighter lanes. Some of you get squeezed out.

It would be pleasant to report that natural selection governs who gets squeezed out, that the fittest remain and the less fit fall by the wayside. But it isn't necessarily merit or competence or performance that rules; merit, competence, and performance are a given. In fact, let's be clear from the very outset that you have the generalist skills or specialist training required in your organization. We will just assume that you have the skills needed to do your job in your organization—and to do it well.

But doing the job well is not going to be enough to win in today's competitive realities. It takes a good deal more to make a successful competitor, one who not only survives the squeeze but sprints ahead of the pack and sets a new standard of speed.

But how? How do you compete to win? How do you make sure that as the road narrows and there's less and less room to maneuver, you're one of the ones who will emerge from the bottleneck, step on the gas, and join the lead cars on the career highway? That's what this chapter is about.

WHAT IT WILL TAKE

Every organization has a different definition of what constitutes success and different criteria for gaining a competitive edge. Obviously, there's no point competing for the criteria of an organization other than your own, so the first task is to understand your organization's criteria for success.

TASK 1: IDENTIFY THE CRITERIA FOR COMPETITIVE SUCCESS

To obtain the pertinent data for this task—that is, to figure out how your particular organization measures success—take a look at the pay scale. Who gets paid the most—and why? Some organizations value certain functions above others. Proctor & Gamble, for instance, was legendary as a marketing organization. Sure, the financial controllers and operations gurus and general managers were all considered important, but the marketing folks were the cream—and they got paid accordingly. In short, if you were going to make it at the old Proctor & Gamble, you had to get into marketing one way or another—and you had to shine there.

In other organizations, it isn't so much a question of function as of operating style. Are bonuses given for demonstrating good teamwork or for individual achievement—or for both?

Do the most highly paid competitors in your organization display or possess a certain something extra that makes them stand out—superior expertise or intelligence, something exotic in their background, some particular achievement or even personality characteristic that distinguishes them?

Write it all down here as you identify what pays at your organization.

COMPETITIVE SUCCESS IN MY ORGANIZATION: WHAT PAYS?

In My Organization, the . . .	What Functions and/or Divisions Get Rewarded?	What Operating Style (Individual vs. Teamwork) Gets Rewarded?	What Other Behaviors Are Rewarded?
Highest Pay Goes to:			
Highest Bonuses Go to:			
Best Assignments Go to:			
Recognition Goes to:			

But don't look only at pay scale. Check out who sits at the right hand of the chairperson, who are the bright stars obviously being groomed for advancement, who is making the speeches and writing the articles that get the company's name in the news. Determine what it is these people are doing or what it is about them that has brought them these markers of success.

COMPETITIVE SUCCESS IN MY
ORGANIZATION: OTHER FACTORS

Names of Successful Competitors in My Organization	Connected	Rising Stars	Names in the News	Other	Reason for Their Success

Add together the information from both charts, and drill down through it to come up with a definition of competitive success at your organization:

_____

_____

_____

_____

WHERE DO YOU STAND?

If these are the criteria for gaining the competitive edge, do you meet the criteria? If not, you'll have to take steps to do so. That's what the next two tasks are about.

TASK 2: MEASURE YOURSELF AGAINST YOUR ORGANIZATION'S CRITERIA FOR COMPETITIVE SUCCESS

How do you measure up to these criteria? Where do you stand on the pay scale? Are you in the "wrong" function? Are there any points of commonality—or could there be—between you and that guy who is always giving speeches at key conferences?

Put it all together here:

CRITERIA FOR COMPETITIVE SUCCESS IN MY ORGANIZATION: HOW DO I MEASURE UP?

	Where do I stand? on a scale of 1 to 5 (low to high)	Why?
Function		
Operating Style		
Connections		
Rising Star		
Name in the News		
Other Behaviors		

Finally, what can you do about all this? Where you don't measure up, should you try to? Should you try to expand on the characteristics or achievements you have in common with the organization's top competitors?

TASK 3: DETERMINE THE ABILITIES YOU'LL NEED TO SPUR AHEAD IN THE COMPETITION

Some people are born winners, with an innate vision they can see and articulate and an inherent ability to realize the vision. But some of the most effective winners on earth were not bred for championship; rather, they developed the abilities needed over time and through experience.

Call it the Seabiscuit syndrome. It's proof that winning can be studied and mastered, and that there is a learning curve for gaining a winning style. If a horse can do it, so

> Personality can open doors, but only character can keep them open.
> —ELMER G. LETTERMAN

can you. Here's what you'll need to do to distinguish yourself from the other vehicles on the road, jump out of the pack, and spurt ahead . . .

Know. If there is a need for expertise beyond the basics discussed at the beginning of this chapter—specialist technical skills and generalist management skills—go get them! Take a course, or apprentice yourself to someone who knows how, or read the right books, but gain the knowledge needed.

Start here and now. Right here, write down those disciplines or subjects you need to know more about:

_____

_____

Communicate. Nothing makes more of a difference than being able to communicate clearly and concisely with those you work with and for, and with those who work for you. The most spectacular achievements can be muddied—and lost—if no one knows they happened or if they are miscommunicated. Clarity in communicating, on the other hand, is the best way to get others to go along with you—and to follow where you lead.

How well do you believe you communicate?

_____

_____

What do you need to improve to communicate better?

_____

_____

Listen. As important as speaking is listening. In fact, we think of this capability as the motor oil of success in an organization. The reason? It lubricates all the parts of life in the organization. Nothing is better guaranteed to smooth the path to a competitive edge. So listen carefully and well.

How are your listening skills? Assess them here: How good a listener are you, and where and how do you need to listen better?

_____

_____

Have Courage. There's a great difference between conviction and orneriness, but when you are sure about what you believe in, have the courage to say so and behave accordingly. Even if what you advocate is unpopular—and even if it turns out to be wrong—taking the lead on something because you truly believe in it is the mark of a bold competitor.

Think about that now. Have you demonstrated courage? How? If not, would you know how to show courage if you had to?

_____

_____

Show Confidence. The best way to convince people you can be trusted is to trust them yourself. That requires a positive belief in your own abilities and beliefs. We're not talking about swagger, but about a sense of what's realistic and an understanding of what you can control and what you cannot control.

When did you last demonstrate confidence in yourself and/or in others?

_____

_____

Take the Initiative. The dictionary defines *initiative* not just as an opening move but also as the "ability to . . . follow through energetically with a plan or task."[1] Both are essential. We're all tired of that guy in the meeting who spouts one daring idea after another—but has no gumption for getting any of his ideas off the ground, much less getting them done. If it's worth starting, it's worth seeing through—and those who do so will definitely stand out from the pack.

What's your initiative score? How and when did you last take the initiative? Write it down here:

_____

_____

Get Involved Externally. It's amazing how doing something important outside the organization makes you look important inside the organization. Involvement in your community, in a local or national charity, or in an event that seemingly has nothing to do with the office can get you noticed at the office. Tally it up. What have you been involved in externally?

_____

_____

Where do you stand in the Seabiscuit syndrome? What do you need to add to your own list of capabilities to put yourself in your organization's victory lane? Is it a matter of formal study, informal observation, or just practice? Look over the answers you gave above, and put together your plan here:

THE SEABISCUIT SYNDROME:
LEARN HOW TO WIN

Winning By:	What Do I Need to Add?	What Do I Need to Do That I Am Not Doing?
Knowing		
Communicating		
Listening		
Having Courage		
Showing Confidence		
Taking the Initiative		
Getting Involved Externally		

WHAT WILL YOU DO TO WIN—
AND WHAT WON'T YOU DO?

It's time to consider how much competitive success is worth to you. You'll measure its worth in what you will and will not do to get it. So before you gun your motor and peel out of the parking lot, think a bit about that famous line—the one you will not cross.

Way back at Road Sign 1, Stop, we told you about Bill's brush with a corporate culture in which fudging the issue was considered a tactical tool. When Bill was ordered to participate in that, he found he simply could not: it was the line he wouldn't cross.

To gain a competitive edge, you're about to try to beat out colleagues. Clearly, only some of you will emerge after the squeeze. People you like may not make it with you. It's important to understand that in competing against these people, you are not violating the bonds of friendship. Also, you're not hoping for anyone else to fail but only for you yourself to succeed.

It is not a game. It is serious stuff. But it is *healthy* competition. If and when you find the competition becomes unhealthy, don't cross that line.

WHAT'S HEALTHY?

While attending a Boston Symphony concert one evening, and thinking about possible competition among the musicians, consultant Richard Karash mused that competition is healthy if it meets three tests:

1. The performance comparisons are clear—i.e., everyone is judged the same.

---

2. The performance comparisons are generally accepted as fair—i.e., not unobtainable.
3. There is a win-win element—i.e., the whole orchestra sounds better, or the whole organization works better.

Richard Karash is a consultant and facilitator covering the broad range of Learning Organization disciplines, with special emphasis on Systems Thinking. He consults, leads meetings, develops and conducts training programs, and delivers speeches and corporate events for a wide range of organizations.

SUMMARY

1. Identify the criteria for competitive success.
2. Measure yourself against your organization's criteria for competitive success.
3. Determine the abilities and capabilities you'll need to spurt ahead in the competition.

Control Your Speed:
Romantic Involvement in the Office

Janice: Is love in the office still prevalent?

Bill: It is prevalent, and it is dangerous. Romantic involvements can have both people losing.

Janice: But work is where most people meet. How can a company stop coworkers from becoming romantically involved?

Bill: They can't, of course. The problem is that such relationships at the office are always noticed, even if you think they're not, and the consequences can be difficult. Employees who become romantically involved could be caught in a real car wreck!

Janice: Yes, and of course the nature of the consequences depends on the culture of your organization, its rules, and the reporting relationship, if any, between the two people.

Bill: Right. It's essential for those involved or about to become an item to evaluate the situation and figure out who will have to give up what if the relationship is to continue, and whether both parties stand to lose equally. That is not usually the case.

Janice: And as we know from our previous book,[1] women generally stand to lose more.

THE OFFICE ROMANCE

Tom and Sandy had enormous respect for each other. Both were professionals par excellence, and though Sandy reported to Tom and was thus a step below him in the hierarchy, the two enjoyed a genuine meeting of the minds where the job was concerned. Both were single-mindedly focused on growing the business, and both were in agreement about the substantive changes that would be needed to meet their growth goals.

To focus on the plans for those changes—without the buzz of office life to distract them—the two began to meet together off-site. They would breakfast together early in the morning—their heads close together as they bounced ideas off each other—then meet again at the end of the day to continue their work.

They made no attempt to hide their time together—nor did they discuss with other colleagues what they were up to. They saw no reason to do either; they were at work. In fact, they were hard at work—and the result of their long but productive time together was a comprehensive plan for rethinking, restructuring, and rejuvenating the division.

But their coworkers knew nothing about the plan. They saw a man and a woman focused intently on each other and spending an inordinate amount of time together, away from the office premises. It had all the earmarks of an affair, and that's exactly what people assumed was going on. In fact, by the time Tom's 360 performance review rolled around, eight out of ten of his direct reports openly said that they believed their married boss, Tom, was romantically involved with their married colleague, Sandy.

It wasn't true, but the very appearance of a romantic involvement was enough to adversely impact Tom's credibility around the organization, his ability to lead, and his overall effectiveness.

Morale among his staff hit a new low. Why work hard if the boss was smitten by a court favorite and had no interest in anyone or anything else? Gossip up and down the corridors took up far more time—and stirred far more interest—than the work itself. The board felt it had no choice but to ask Tom to tender his resignation—all for a perception that had no basis in fact.

But here's the ironic twist to the story. In their shared anger and disappointment over Tom's dismissal, Tom and Sandy grew even closer. Sandy decided to follow Tom out of the organization. Faster than either of them thought possible, the two fell in love, and the once baseless rumors at last came true. Both marriages broke up, families were sundered, and Tom and Sandy married and relocated. The company, meanwhile, having lost the services of two fine professionals—as well as the excellent plan they had worked out in those months off-site—continued to go downhill.

Bottom line? Everyone lost.

The lesson to be drawn from all this is a simple but far too often painful one: romantic relationships with coworkers have consequences. This is a danger zone. If you drive into it, do so with your eyes wide open.

CODES AND PRECEDENTS

We're all adults here, so let's be clear on what we're talking about: a relationship between two consenting adults. If one of the adults is not consenting, that is something else altogether, but whether the issue is people falling madly in love with each other over a product development plan, or involves one person making unwelcome advances to another, there are codes that should guide conduct, and precedents that signal the consequences.

Task 1: Check Out the Culture and Code at Your Organization and See What Others Have Done— and What Has Happened as a Result

There are still organizations that prohibit "fraternization"—that is, personal relationships—between any two employees under any circumstances. There are others that set down specific rules and regulations concerning possible romances between people in a reporting relationship or at different levels of the hierarchy. Still other organizations may not have *written* rules of conduct, but the code of behavior is so ingrained in the culture that rules exist nevertheless.

Don't wait till they hit you over the head to find out what those rules are. Seek out the facts today. If the code wasn't included in your orientation kit or isn't in the employee handbook or cannot be found in the manual of policies and procedures, check with Human Resources. It's important to be clear about what will be expected of you if and when the thunderbolt of passion strikes you—or someone who has targeted you as the object of his or her passion.

One way to figure it out is to see what has happened to people in the organization who have been involved in office relationships. Ask around, learn their stories, and find out how the stories ended. Were there dismissals and departures, as in the case of Tom and Sandy? Or did all end well for all involved? The answers should tell you what you need to know before you head into the danger zone of romance on the job.

BEHAVIOR TIPS FOR THE DANGER ZONE

While it is true that many folks fall in love with people they meet at work, other men and women work side by side together for years without ever becoming romantically entangled. And that's how men and women really should behave at the office—like people who are working together without becoming romantically entangled, even if they are.

TASK 2: MAKE SURE YOUR BEHAVIOR IS PROFESSIONAL AT ALL TIMES—AND THAT YOU ARE NOT GIVING OFF THE WRONG SIGNALS

This is an office, not a disco. It's a place of work, not of play. Everyone should dress, act, and speak accordingly. If someone does *not* dress, act, and speak accordingly, and it adversely impacts you, you may have to take action to either get out of the situation or shut the person down. But remember that you, too, are responsible for dressing, acting, and speaking in a manner that is at all times absolutely professional.

There is a simple reality when it comes to life at the office: whatever you do or say there will eventually become known. Tom and Sandy forgot that salient point, with dire results. It was pretty foolish of the two of them not to communicate openly to their colleagues about their off-site meetings; it was downright dumb to be seen breakfasting together, heads bent toward each other in intent conversation. And it was really stupid for them to head off to their off-site meetings at the end of the workday—in plain sight of their peers, subordinates, and supervisors. For remember: it was the appearance of an affair, not an actual affair, that led to their downfall.

True, it was perhaps equally foolish of Tom and Sandy's coworkers to make assumptions about the behavior they saw—especially since the assumptions were unfounded. But fair or not, assumptions *are* made.

Assumptions are made if a woman wears suggestive clothing—and if a man comments on it.

Assumptions are made if a certain kind of off-color or salacious humor is expressed—and if you laugh at it.

Assumptions are made if someone tells you the sad tale of his marriage—and you listen to it sympathetically.

Assumptions are made if a man and woman manage all too frequently to "find themselves" alone together.

Assumptions are made if you say too much about where you'll be at what time—in case someone wants to call you or find you.

Dismissing some of these actions as meaningless or "just kidding around" or in no way harmful can be hazardous. For one thing, maybe the joke you told was meaningless to you, but to the guy from IT, it sounded like an invitation. Maybe you look upon listening to a tale of a bad marriage as simple human kindness, but the fellow with the bad marriage has a lot more to say, and he'd like to say it to you alone, in private, maybe in the bar after work. Behavior that is out of place can all too easily be misinterpreted.

Carve the rule in stone: stick to business when in the office. That means dressing, speaking, and behaving in a businesslike way.

Ditto if the two of you are madly in love. Keep it out of the office. Clearly, work is a social stage, and it can be fun to joke and interact with coworkers. That's precisely how coworkers fall in love. But once you do fall in love, take it home. Your romance simply doesn't belong on the job. The cardinal rule is "Keep your personal life personal." It does not belong in the office.

WHEN THE ADVANCE IS UNWELCOME

Karen was thrilled when her boss asked her to dinner. She was new to the organization, had been assigned a difficult and sensitive task, and was pretty sure this was going to be a working dinner to discuss strategy and tactics.

She was wrong. The boss's intention in taking Karen to dinner was something else altogether. Simply put, his plan was that Karen would be the dessert, as he made perfectly clear as soon as the first cocktail was served.

To say the meal was awkward was putting it mildly. Karen was stunned, speechless, and absolutely clueless about how to act or what to do. Should she get up and leave? Should she laugh it off? Should she change the subject? She tried both of the latter two, and nothing worked. For his part, the boss was also stunned. After all, the woman had accepted his dinner invitation. That meant she acquiesced, didn't it? Why else did she think he'd asked her to dinner? To talk about the project? That wasn't for dinner; that was for the office.

It was a fast, quiet meal. Karen stumbled and fumbled, searching for benign things to say. The boss just wanted to get out of the restaurant without making too much of a scene. When they parted after the meal, he was unsmiling and unspeaking.

He maintained that attitude in the office. Karen was completely dumbfounded; she had no idea what to do next. Her boss wasn't talking to her or paying her the slightest attention; her career was suspended in midair; and she hadn't done anything wrong. Then one day a veteran manager took her aside and filled her in on the classic mantra about love at the office: "Breakfast is for business," the woman told Karen, "lunch is for selling, and dinner is private."

It's a good working mantra. Had Karen said no to the dinner, the boss would likely have tried again, and another no would probably have put an end to his interest. She compounded her own folly, once the damage was done and the boss had been both shot down and embarrassed, by failing to confront the situation at the office after the fact. It would have been wise for her to ask for a meeting at the office to clear the air—and to do this, if possible, with humor and goodwill.

When behavior is abusive, disrespectful, and detrimental to one's career, it should not be tolerated. It's also illegal. What did the notorious "Boom Boom Room" cost Smith Barney when the women who had to put up with its sexist and raunchy behavior brought a class action suit? How about Morgan Stanley's $45 million settlement? Merrill Lynch's $100 million payout? Or UBS, Europe's biggest bank, which gave $29 million to a single individual suing on the charge of sex discrimination? All paid dearly when they lost class action suits and individual lawsuits filed on grounds of sexual harassment and discrimination. Intolerable, illegal, and expensive: that is a no-win situation for the harasser and discriminator and for those who tolerate harassment and discrimination.

TASK 3: DEFLECT UNWELCOME ADVANCES AS LONG AS YOU CAN; THEN TAKE ACTION

But you don't start with a lawsuit. You start by deflecting unwelcome advances. Humor, in fact, is one of the best ways to do so. Laugh it off; better yet, pretend the person making the unwanted advance was just kidding. It was a joke; nobody meant anything bad by it; let's both rewind to where we were a moment ago. Then get right back to business.

If the person persists in the unwanted advances, a good round rejection is very much in order: "Absolutely not!" "I am not interested." "The answer is no!" Any or all of these should make it perfectly clear that this is not going to happen.

If that doesn't work, you'll have to take action. For one thing, the unwanted advances may well constitute harassment. Whatever your reporting relationship, if any, with the person making the advances, the law says that "continued, unwelcome sexual advances" in the workplace may fit the definition of sexual harassment, which is a form of discrimination, and illegal. So if it continues, report it to your supervisor (unless the supervisor is the offender, of course) or to the human resources department. If you get no satisfaction from any of these, see a lawyer. You don't have to take harassment.

Make sure that during the course of events, you keep notes on what transpires, however minor an action or a behavior may seem. Note the date and time of an incident, write down the comments made or behaviors exhibited, and report what action you took to mitigate the unwanted advances.

The bottom line, harassment is illegal and must stop. Period. For everything else, whether mild flirtation or profound love, when in the office, stick to business. When off the premises, that's your business . . .

SUMMARY

The office is not the place for love, romance, or flirtation. It's the place for work. But since you can't always choose the time and place for love, romance, or flirtation, make sure you do the following:

1. Check out the culture and code at your organization and see what others have done—and what has happened as a result.
2. Make sure your behavior is professional at all times—and that you are not giving off the wrong signals.
3. Deflect unwelcome advances as long as you can; then take action.

Caution: Family Matters

Janice: Family matters, particularly children, can create major potholes on the career highway. Children take time, effort, energy, and all your focus. And if it is not children, these days it can often be elder care. Handling family responsibilities and a full-time career is tricky!

Bill: Yes, and either way, that sometimes means time away from the career. Any time you do that—any time you take substantial time off from the career to attend to family matters—at most companies, there is going to be a price to pay. And it can be very difficult to come back.

Janice: I see this often in my work with women who have taken time out to have kids. They've been off the career highway four, five, maybe even ten years, and there's no way they can simply waltz back into the professional job market and pick up where they left off.

Bill: The world may have changed multiple times while they've been away. Their skills and training may be entirely outdated. They try to start over, but now they're competing against people just out of business school—candidates with the very latest knowledge and training. Time away can be costly.

Janice: On the other hand, there is a huge personal price to pay if you don't attend to family responsibilities, and we've both seen what that can do to people.

Bill: Absolutely. Kids in trouble, family life unraveling: you can't let these responsibilities go.

CAN YOU HAVE IT ALL?

The short answer is yes, but you're going to need help. It's difficult almost to the point of impossibility to have both a full-time career and be a full-time parent if you're on your own. So if you're in a relationship with someone who does not share your interest in having both family and career, think hard about committing to that relationship.

It could perhaps be argued that for generations, men had it all. They went out each morning to a job that presumably brought its share of satisfactions, then returned home each evening to a well-tended home filled with well-tended children—or what at least appeared to be well-tended children. The men had the option of spending a fair amount of quality time with those children; they enjoyed freedom from household responsibilities as the trade-off for their breadwinning duties.

Then women tried to have it all too, and that's where the problems came in—especially when some people began to blame the women themselves. But the fact was that if both parents left the house each morning to seek satisfaction and rewards in the workplace, the home and the children were less well tended.

Something had to give. Something had to change.

Corporate America is on the threshold of that change today, as companies have learned the hard way that they don't want to miss out on the talents and potential achievements of women—and some men—torn between their desire and/or need to work and their responsibilities as parents.

Some women have opted out of the corporate workforce altogether, choosing to keep their talents home with their children. A great many others have opted out of corporate organizations; instead, they seek to create or join small, entrepreneurial businesses that are home based, where they can be flexible about their time and their workloads. There's even a new word for these stay-at-home-but-stay-in-business women: *mompreneurs*. They don't have to fight traffic, office politics, the glass ceiling, or one another if they stay at or near the house, use the latest technologies to do business, and arrange their days such that their children are nearby, if not underfoot.

No wonder more and more women of childbearing age are becoming mompreneurs. According to the Center for Women's Business Research, from 1997 to 2004, the number of women-owned businesses rose 17 percent; during the same time period, the number of all businesses starting up rose a mere 9 percent.[1] So when corporations wonder where their talented women workers went, one answer is that they went into business—and went home to do it.

Corporate America is certainly feeling the pinch. The loss of some of the best and brightest in the American workforce—highly educated, highly motivated women representing that portion of the population most responsible for key consumer buying decisions—is a loss corporations cannot afford. More and more of them are innovating programs that build in flexibility about how and where people may work and how they may keep their connections to a company from a distance. It's an indication that companies recognize and value the talent of these women, and that they don't want to lose out on the contributions they expect these women will make to the companies over the course of their career.

We're going to see more and more of this. In 2005, the Simmons School of Management and The Committee of 200, an organization of women business leaders, conducted a survey of young girls and boys about career expectations.[2] Among the girls, 82 percent said they expected to work full-time, and 97 percent said they expected to provide financially for themselves and their families. The boys had similar expectations. It won't be long until these boys and girls are on the job. It also won't be long before they find one another, marry, and begin families. And the best of them will gravitate to those organizations that make it easier for them both to keep their place in a profession and give their best to their families.

A FAMILY AFFAIR

How do you mesh your responsibilities at home and your responsibilities at the office in a way that does justice to both? It's a question women and men have wrestled with for a very long time. In this chapter, we offer some pretty simple guidelines to answer the question, but we add these caveats: doing right by both responsibilities is a family affair, and it requires all members of the family to make some compromises, if not sacrifices.

The best place to start, however, is by thinking through the issue, and that requires getting all the facts you can.

TASK 1: BEFORE YOU HAVE CHILDREN, DO THE RESEARCH: ISSUES, OPTIONS, COSTS, BENEFITS

Are you ready to start a family? What might it mean to your career—and to your relationship to your career? To find out, do the research. What we mean is research the issues, your options, what it all might cost—not just financially—and whether you think the benefits are worth the costs.

For example, when is the right time to start a family—in terms of both personal well-being and the well-being of your career? If you're a woman, should you wait until you've achieved the promotion to vice president or higher before you take maternity leave to have or adopt a child? What will be the impact if you take the leave right after being appointed to a higher position? What are the risks of waiting to have or adopt a child?

Talk to your doctor, of course, but check with other women as well. This is not an untrodden path, so find out how that woman in marketing did it—after all, she's about your age. Talk to some of the older women about potential prob-

> The thing that impresses me the most about America is the way parents obey their children.
>
> —EDWARD, DUKE OF WINDSOR, 1894–1972

lems, conflicts, and the like. You should also check out policies, procedures, and precedents at your company. The point is to do all you can to understand what you may be getting into and what will change once a baby arrives.

If you're a man, you're not off the hook. What is your company's policy about paternity leave—and when would be the best time for you to take such leave? The best possible scenario would be one in which you and your spouse are in sync on the best time to start a family—that is, when the time that's best for her is best for you and, above all, is also best for the child you both want to have. Such a scenario may not be possible, but by doing substantive research ahead of time, you may at least have a chance to come close.

FAMILY PLAN

In your due diligence in Task 1 about starting a family, you probably learned that children change everything—absolutely everything. To make sure you can handle the change—and that it won't derail your career ambitions—you need a plan.

TASK 2: CREATE A DETAILED PLAN TO DEAL WITH THE DUAL RESPONSIBILITY OF A CHILD AND A CAREER

Jack and Molly had been in no hurry to start a family. Both were focused on their careers, and both found enormous satisfaction in their work and in their steady rise up the corporate hierarchy. But when Jack turned forty and Molly was in her late thirties, they decided they'd better have a child now, before it was too late. And without a firm plan in place, to their surprise, a baby was on the way.

Of course, the baby was a blessing and a joy to them both—and a revelation as well. They had thought ahead, but not successfully planned, what they would do after Molly's three-month maternity leave was over—and Molly, juggling work from home while trying to deal with a newborn, couldn't wait till she could get back to work. But both of them were stunned at what a professional nanny would charge to take care of the baby full-time, and while a good local day care carried a more reasonable price, neither of them particularly liked the idea of turning the baby over to a group situation. Moreover, neither of them kept what could be called "regular hours." With day care, at least one of them would have to be on the spot on time to pick up the baby. Was this going to be possible? Their commute was fairly long, and they lived in the Northeast, where winters could be treacherous. What if the roads were closed or sloppy and they simply couldn't get back to the baby when they were supposed to?

And above all, why hadn't they thought about all this ahead of time?

Let's be clear: caring for children is the most important responsibility you have. Weigh the product development meeting against getting your kid to the doctor, and it's no contest—no contest at all. But even though you're a parent, you're also a professional—and you have obligations at the office as well as at home. The best way to fulfill both sets of obligations is with a plan.

Start with the economics. Do you have the financial wherewithal to pay for a nanny? Day care? Some combination of the two? If not, what provision will you make for your child during the day—and what will that mean for your work situation?

Even with professional help, however, you still need backup; that is, someone needs to be designated the primary caregiver. By primary caregiver, we mean the person who will drop everything, whatever it is, if and when the child becomes ill, the nanny has to take time off, or the babysitter fails to show up.

Your backup also needs backup. Plan for somebody nearby who can fill in for a little bit of time, if needed, till the primary caregiver can take over.

A child changes the dynamic in the household in all sorts of ways—the dynamic between parents as well as the dynamic if there are other children already on the scene. Plan for these possible changes as well.

After all, you're a professional. Planning is a skill you're trained in, a skill you've honed on the job. Your most important job in life is coming up—parenthood. It deserves the best plan you can manage. Here's a template that will help:

Basic Factors to Be Considered	Other Options	Solutions
Financial Implications • Single income • No income for a while • Savings • Potential unexpected costs for twins, sick child, elder care, etc.		
Nanny/Caregiver • Cost • Comfort with person		
Backup Care • Family • Friend • Another nanny		
Household Accommodations • Space for child • Space for nanny • Space for home office • Space for other needs		
Communication Issues		
Doctor Support and Location		
Other Issues		

By the way, the dilemma Jack and Molly faced was resolved in an interesting way. Although Molly loved her baby unreservedly, at thirty-eight, she found motherhood something of a drain on her time and her energy, and the idea of spending all day every day with the baby was simply not appealing. Jack, on the other hand, was enthralled with fatherhood. Weary of the infighting at his company, he suggested becoming the stay-at-home parent; although they would lose his salary, they would not have to pay for full-time care for the baby—and it was something he wanted to do. It was the perfect solution: both parents got what they wanted, and their son got the full-time care and attention of one loving parent, plus the benefit of two parents who loved both him and their careers.

Although we've both managed careers and families, we don't pretend to be experts on how to do it. But plenty of people are, and many of them have written books on the subject. Browse your local library or bookstore for more on this subject, and for an even more exhaustive checklist of the changes that new parents must consider, plan for, and deal with.

FAMILY LEAVE

You may be eligible under the Family and Medical Leave Act (FMLA) to take 12 weeks of unpaid leave after the birth or adoption of a child—with a guarantee that you will come back to your old job or to a similar position with equivalent compensation, benefits, working conditions, and seniority.

Do you work for the federal, state, or local government, or for a company with 50 or more employees working within 75 miles of the workplace? If so, you're eligible.

Have you worked for your employer for at least 12 months, and have you put in an average of 25 hours per week for 50 weeks during the previous year? If so, you're eligible.

Talk to your human resources department for more details.

DANGER: BURNING BRIDGE

One crisp autumn day, Janice received an inquiry from a woman who had been head of marketing for the consumer products division of a major corporation—twelve years ago! She had "taken time off," as she put it, to have three children, and now she was ready to get back into the workplace. What could Janice do for her? And could Janice see her immediately?

Twelve years is several lifetimes in the business world. Think of it: a dozen years ago, cell phones were unusual, BlackBerrys were unheard of, and Six Sigma was an idea embraced by only a few corporate leaders. The entire way of doing business was different twelve years ago. The kinds of goals and objectives organizations set for themselves were different, as were the skills and training required. The idea that an individual could go away for twelve years and step back in, picking up where she had left off, was unimaginable. Yet this woman was convinced that her outstanding achievements of more than a decade back would be welcomed by most companies. She was wrong. It's an essential lesson—and an essential task in managing the parent trap.

Task 3: Keep the Connection to the World of Work

We can't recommend this strongly enough. If you intend to return to work, don't drop out of the corporate world entirely when you take up parenting. Keep some sort of connection. If you don't, you run the risk of burning your bridge back to the corporate world as an employee—even as a consultant.

What kind of connection? Try working out some sort of from-home consulting contract with your company. Or start your own home venture, like those mompreneurs we talked about earlier. Or, if you can, work part-time; it may even be worth it if your compensation for part-time work is eaten up by paying for a babysitter, just so you can keep the connection to the working world as a temp for an agency, on a company payroll, or as a freelancer. You can even volunteer your time to a for-profit or not-for-profit organization just to stay current with what's happening inside organizations and keep a finger on the pulse of the professional life.

That's what Janice recommended to the woman who had taken off twelve years to have kids: to accept something temporary— to accept *anything*—as a way to reestablish herself in the world of work, and to catch up with the changes that had taken place in the time she was away. "Go through your rolodex," Janice advised her. "Call your former bosses, colleagues, and others, and find a part-time or freelance position using your best talent"—in her case, writing—"to make a contribution, get noticed, and get hired." She connected with a former colleague, did freelance work, was hired on a part-time basis, and is now full-time as an assistant marketing director for an investment management firm. She had the skills; she just needed to bring them up to date and prove her value.

One exciting development is that many corporations are reaching out to their former women employees—who have left for a variety of personal reasons—and are offering them the opportunity to "come back" and work full-time, part-time, or, most interestingly, on a flex-time basis. If your corporation is thus enlightened, be sure you keep the connection to see how you might reenter a workplace where they already know you, know your capabilities, and may embrace your return. This is a mutually beneficial opportunity: companies have access to talent they know, while women in particular don't feel forced to opt out of their careers to take care of very real needs.

> One of the symptoms of an approaching nervous breakdown is the belief that one's work is terribly important.
>
> —BERTRAND RUSSELL, BRITISH AUTHOR, MATHEMATICIAN, AND PHILOSOPHER, 1872–1970

PRIORITIES

It may be a cliché, but it's worth repeating: nobody ever goes to the grave wishing they'd spent more time at the office. Your work is important: it gives you choices you might not otherwise have, and— we hope—it enriches your life. Some people work for the money, some for power, some for social interaction, some for the toys they can accumulate, and others because it's part of their DNA. And for some, it is a means to an end. But for most people, when they do a reality check, it is not the most important thing in the world.

PRIORITY CHART

Rate what really drives you—what makes you get up in the morning and go to work: 1–19 (1 being most important)

_____	Money	_____	Travel
_____	Power	_____	Office
_____	Social interaction	_____	Being viewed as an expert
_____	Recognition	_____	Being wanted/included
_____	Intellectual stimulation	_____	Being involved
_____	Corporate toys	_____	Subordinates
_____	Overall relationships	_____	Boss
_____	The work itself/achievements	_____	Peers
_____	Status or title	_____	Clients
_____	Other:_____		

Rate your Personal Priorities: 1–12 (1 being most important). Cross out those that do not apply.

_____	Significant other/Spouse	_____	Civic responsibility
_____	Children	_____	Board/Association work
_____	Parents		
_____	Siblings	_____	Extracurricular activities
_____	Church	_____	Your physical, personal, professional needs
_____	Charitable work		
_____	Friends	_____	Other: _____

What do you see about yourself as you look at this list? What counts for you?

Task 4: Spend Time with Your Children

Yes, this is a cliché as well, and we're sorry to be preaching it, but both of us in our work see people who have forgotten how very important it is to spend time with their children. Smart, talented, extremely accomplished people. And they regret it later. Always.

The highway sign is very clear on the subject: slow down; there are children here. Reduce the corporate go-go juice. Yes, it can be exciting. The work is rewarding; the competition can be thrilling; even the anxiety can be exhilarating. But at the end of the day, what really counts? Aren't your friends, your hobbies, your faith, and, above all, your family what it's all about? When that inner voice tells you you're missing some part of your children's lives even as you race ahead on the career highway, listen hard. Slow down. Those people you are passing by on the side of the road are your children.

SUMMARY

How can you give your best to both your career and your family?

1. Before you have children, do the research: issues, options, costs, benefits.
2. Create a detailed plan for dealing with the dual responsibility of a child and a career.
3. Keep the connection to the world of work.
4. Spend time with your children.

```
┌─────────────────┐
│ ┌─────────────┐ │
│ │  EMERGENCY  │ │
│ │  STOPPING   │ │
│ │    ONLY     │ │
│ └─────────────┘ │
└─────────────────┘
```

Integrate Life and Work: Resume Speed

Bill: Ever feel like all the personal aspects of your life are taking over your career, and that so much is going on that you just have to pull over and stop?

Janice: Absolutely. Who doesn't? We keep hearing about work/life balance. Totally wrong. It will never happen. What we need to do is *integrate* work and life if we can—and sometimes it is questionable.

Bill: Exactly. You can't pull over for personal life; if you do, the world will pass you right by.

Janice: You know, you spend maybe twelve hours a day on the job— maybe even more time thinking about work. Work becomes your life.

THE WORK/LIFE IMBALANCE

Overbusy? Overburdened? Overwhelmed?

You know what? Who isn't?

We all have personal lives, and not a single one of them is perfect; that's a given. The problem comes when personal needs take their toll on your professional life.

The opposite is true as well: your professional life can take a toll on your personal life. Either way, your career—and your life—can be thrown off track, and soon enough, you find that both have come to a screeching halt in the ditch at the side of the road. But such emergency stopping can be dangerous: all the other cars are whizzing past you; the ditch may be tough to climb out of; the car may be hard to start after that abrupt braking; and you may be too shaken to drive. So emergency stopping is to be avoided at all costs—except when absolutely necessary.

The issue for your career, therefore, is being able to stay on track when personal needs so interfere with work that they threaten to knock you off the road. Even if the need morphs into a crisis, it's essential to stay on the road and stay moving. The question is how. How do you keep from having to pull over and stop—especially if and when stopping may seriously jeopardize your ability to start up again?

The first answer is that there are crises and there are *crises*. Some needs really do take precedence over everything else, while others are simply part of the ebb and flow of existence. Janice recently handled a candidate search process that had both types of needs—and both were experienced by the same job candidate. Call him Robert, a very promising candidate for a major position that required relocation. Early on in the course of the recruitment process, Janice learned that Robert's brother was in the last stages of terminal cancer.

"How can you go on?" she asked him when he told her the facts.

"If I didn't have this job opportunity to focus on," Robert replied, "I'd lose it altogether."

It sounded entirely reasonable; Janice could easily understand how concentrating on his own bright future might lift Robert from his involvement with illness and death, raise his spirits, remind him that life does go on.

But then came the phone call Janice had been dreading. Robert's brother had died, and Robert was calling an end to his recruitment.

"I really have to stop now," he said. "I need to take the time to grieve for my brother." Again, she understood. They both knew that Robert's career would suffer from the loss of this opportunity, but they both also knew that right now, career opportunity was not what counted in Robert's life.

It is a standard most of us recognize when we see it. A parent or spouse or sibling or child in need of our constant focus requires emergency stopping; you cannot walk away from such a need, and you would find it utterly impossible to try to do so. But anything and everything short of that standard is simply part of daily life, no matter how distressing or depressing or disturbing or enraging or exhilarating it may be—and it's essential to deal with it without sacrificing your work or losing your place in line.

The second answer to the question of how to keep from pulling over for an emergency stop at every crisis or need is this: integrate the personal and the professional. They don't belong apart anyway. After all, life is not a collection of fragments you can stash in different compartments. As Janice noted at the top of this chapter, you spend some twelve hours a day at work—a third of your life. This *is* your life: the personal and the professional together, unified into an integrated whole.

> A human being must have occupation if he or she is not to become a nuisance to the world.
>
> —Dorothy L. Sayers,
> British writer,
> 1893–1957

The two are, in fact, as essential to each other as two sides of a coin. You seek satisfaction in both; you derive satisfaction from achievements in both; the satisfaction you derive gives you pleasure, enhances your life—without regard to whether it comes from the month's sales figures at the office or the healthy children in the home. Each one enriches the other; both make you the person you are.

Back at Road Sign 12, you thought long and hard about the choice to start a family so you could integrate life and work in ways that would benefit both. Now you have to learn to do the integrating.

It is therefore past time to stop talking about balancing life and work, because the balance will never be equal; it will shift from one to the other, back and forth and forth and back, as long as you keep the two separate in your mind. Rather, accept that you have one life, not two separate lives—and live your life in an integrated way.

INTEGRATING CONCERN

If you're concerned about your ability to integrate life and work, you're not alone. According to a Rutgers University national poll of 1,000 workers, 97 percent of workers believe "the ability to balance work and family life"—i.e., to integrate the two—is the single most important aspect of their job.[1]

COMPASS POINT

Some people find it easier to live an integrated life than others, no matter how tough things get. Julie is a top-flight consultant with a booming practice. She is also a divorced mother of three young children, two of whom have shown signs of a learning disability. In 2005, the family lost their house and all their possessions to Hurricane Katrina. They were in a shelter for a week, then lived with Julie's sister—Julie used a laptop and a new cell phone to stay in business—then decided to pick up and relocate to the Northeast, where Julie recently closed on a house, which was still unfurnished as of this writing, and put the kids in a new school.

Through it all, Julie remained cool, calm, and collected—not just by outward appearances, but inwardly as well. When asked, "How do you cope?" she had a simple answer: "I just do." Behind that answer lies a straightforward, structured approach: "I make lists, set my priorities for the week and the day—business-related, family-related, and me-related priorities, all together—and if something is going to come between me and my work, I let my clients know." With such an approach as a foundation, Julie has been able to weather short-term crises like losing a home, long-term crises like her kids' disabilities, and overwhelming crises like Katrina, without losing her inner well-being—a compass that keeps her going along her own individual track without having to pull over and stop.

> Work is about daily meaning as well as daily bread.
>
> —STUDS TERKEL, AMERICAN AUTHOR

The issue isn't work or life or hurricanes; the issue is knowing that life is not a smooth, untroubled line from birth to death, that it sometimes plays hardball, and that it often throws knuckleballs you don't see till they whistle past you, low and inside. The real issue is being equipped to catch whatever is pitched, hit them if you can, or in any event, duck in time.

HOW DO YOU DEAL WITH CRISES?

What might constitute a life crisis? The answers are as variegated as the human race. After all, it's your life, so a crisis is whatever disturbs your life enough that it threatens to throw you off track and send you into the emergency stopping zone. Money worries, a broken relationship, family struggles, small-town gossip, the big-city rat race—we all know the things that can potentially tip us over the edge. The issue is how we deal with it.

Some people just withdraw. By isolating themselves and hiding their difficulties, they manage to avoid being hurt. They also cut themselves off from any means of support. Others "cope" by self-medicating in one way or another: alcohol, drugs, overindulgence in "comfort food," and the like. The problem there, of course, is that when they eventually sober up, the crisis has not gone away. There are those who act out their worries through aggressive behavior, but that eventually only isolates them further—and probably adds guilt in the end. And there are those who simply remain locked in a feeling of hopelessness, drifting deeper and deeper into debilitating despair or depression.

Task 1: Assess How You Deal with Crises

Do you know how you tend to deal with a crisis? Put yourself in the following scenarios to find out:

Scenario 1:

Despite an extremely generous salary sufficient to cover your needs and more, you've been consuming above your means and have spent your way into serious "money woes." Your response is to

1. beat up on yourself for your stupidity
2. fly off for a week's vacation to get your mind off your troubles
3. make a plan to work your way out of the financial hole you're in

Scenario 2:

Maybe this is just the seven-year itch, but whatever it is, there's a lot of tension in your marriage right now. As a result, you

1. worry that this is going to end the relationship and lead to divorce
2. pour out your troubles to your best friend
3. have a serious sit-down with your spouse, focusing on the problem and the options for solving it (including seeing a therapist)

Scenario 3:

Merger rumors are rife around the office, and the betting is that the acquiring organization will "win," while your organization will get hammered. You are most likely to

1. move into high-anxiety mode, wondering what you'll do if you're axed
2. take a wait-and-see attitude; after all, these are only rumors
3. talk to your supervisor and devise a strategy for giving yourself the strongest possible position for either surviving or not surviving a merger

If your answers were mostly 1s, chances are your response to crisis in general is to ruminate over it, and this is, of course, important; analysis and self-reflection are key to any kind of decision or action. Too often, however, 1-answering types fail to move past the analysis and self-reflection to the deciding and acting. Or they focus on the negative possibilities. Either way, when thinking becomes obsessing, it's counterproductive.

For Type-1 responders, it's good to keep in mind that when you set an objective, you also need to map out a way to get there. That will help focus your thinking so it doesn't ramble on aimlessly but comes down to earth a bit.

If you are a 2-answer type, you're probably a pretty good escape artist. Again, this has its good points: it is always useful to distract yourself from stressful situations and not take them too seriously. The other side of the coin, however, is denial—in which case you may render yourself incapable of avoiding or averting an impending threat. Type 2s can also so distract themselves with other activities or obsessive/compulsive behavior that they are prone to various forms of addiction.

Type-2 responders would do better to blend their escape artistry with some serious thinking about solutions. While it's important not to be thrown by a crisis, it's also important to rise to the occasion, adapting yourself to the need without being thrown by it.

Those who answered 3 to these scenarios tend to be take-charge kinds of people with a proactive approach to handling crises. You have confidence that the crisis is a problem that, at the very least, you can counter, and at best, you can solve. It's a great way to be—unless and until you come to believe that there's nothing you can't fix, even other people's problems and even situations that in reality are beyond your control.

Sometimes, in fact, the best solution for 3-answer types isn't necessarily to take charge but rather to do something that proves emotionally nurturing. Psychologists call this the tend-and-befriend response to crisis or stress, and it can be as important as solving the crisis itself. It also puts you in a position to look at alternative solutions in case things do not come out as you had planned. After all, the aim, as always, is to avoid any emergency stopping.

STAYING ON TRACK

The best way to avoid emergency stopping, of course, is to anticipate those forces that might throw you off track. That way, you can at least deal with them, even if you can't stop them.

Task 2: Anticipate Potential Crises

To get a handle on potential crises, fill out the following chart. First, list the personal issues that are emerging in your life, even if they seem to be on the back burner for now; these are issues that might conceivably move to the front burner to affect your daily decision making. Then, on a scale of 1 to 5, assess how much each might affect your work, where 1 is the least disruptive and 5 is the most disruptive. Finally, take a hard look at which of these issues should be dealt with *now*, before it becomes a crisis that could send you flying off the road and braking hard.

Personal Issue	COLUMN 1	COLUMN 2
	Potential for Crisis? 1 = Least Probable 5 = Most Probable	Deal with It Today? 1 = Least Essential to Deal with Today 5 = Most Essential to Deal with Today
Child in Need		
Family/Friend in Need		
Job Changing		
Money Issues		
New Home		
Depression		
Physical Concern		
Health Problem		
Other Problem(s)		

TASK 3: PRIORITIZE

Now that you know the potential for crisis, you're in a position to prioritize the requirements of work and home in a way that will let you deal with the crisis as you continue to carry out responsibilities in both arenas.

Structure how you will approach the situation by answering the following questions:

1. What are the issues I face?
2. How much time will I need away from the job to deal with issues at home?
3. How much time will I need away from home to deal with issues on the job?
4. How can I be sure to tend to my personal needs and meet the demands of the job?

PERSONAL ISSUES PRIORITIZED

Personal Issue	Total of Columns 1 and 2 in Prior Chart	Schedule of Dealing with Each Issue
Child in Need		
Family/Friend in Need		
Job Changing		
Money Issues		
New Home		
Depression		
Physical Concern		

Personal Issue	Total of Columns 1 and 2 in Prior Chart	Schedule of Dealing with Each Issue
Health Problem		
Other Problem(s)		

While tending to *personal* needs, I will fulfill the following *professional tasks,* and here's how I'll do it:

Personal Need	Professional Task	How to Fulfill Both

You certainly need to be very clear about your feelings in the midst of a crisis so that you don't, under any circumstances, allow them to intrude into your professional actions. Knowing what your feelings are will enable you to recognize if and when they do begin to intrude—and you can quickly draw the line.

One thing is clear: you can't "lose it" at work. Certainly, you cannot ignore the reality of a true personal crisis, but bringing your personal crisis into the work setting is both unprofessional and inappropriate. If you feel close to losing it, close the door to your office or walk around the block or stay home for a mental-health day; whichever stratagem you choose, the aim is to deal with the personal issue in the personal arena—not in the workplace, where it simply does not belong. If you don't deal with it, you run the risk of having it explode, and that won't help your professional or your personal life.

And here's something else that's important to note: while it is unlikely that you will have two equally critical situations—"true crises"—at any one time, if you do, then you must evaluate whether or not you may just need to take a full emergency stop. That could mean taking time off from the job—in the form of a leave of absence, a sabbatical, or even resigning. Many companies have learned how to be compassionate with employees who face a true crisis in their families; they'll forgive time taken away from the office and will grant employees room to get their lives back in order. Taking time off for a family crisis may also qualify under the Family Leave Act of 1993, which provides twelve weeks of unpaid leave to tend to a crisis that requires your full-time focus. Check with your company HR department about your company's policies regarding this kind of time off.

YOU'RE NOT ALONE

John noticed that Maggie, one of his direct reports, did not seem herself. Normally quick to anticipate his thoughts, sharp in her responses, and thorough in her work, she had lately seemed sluggish, indifferent, even a bit sloppy. He had even had to chew her out for a mistake that was so unlike her that it stunned him more than it angered him. He liked Maggie and worried what this slump might mean to her promotion potential, but he figured it was something personal, and he was uncomfortable prying. Besides, he feared he might be accused of some form of sexual harassment if he appeared to take an interest in how things were going at home or in her marriage. So he let it pass, figuring she would just work it out.

TASK 4: SEEK SUPPORT
You don't have to go through this alone. In fact, it's important to let your boss know that you are going through a troubling time.

That requires trust, and if you don't feel a sufficient level of trust with your supervisor, let *someone* in the organization know—a peer perhaps, or the human resources department, which most likely can refer you to an Employee Assistance Program that may be able to provide expert help.

The reason is simple: personal situations take some time away from work, directly or indirectly, and you do not want this to be misinterpreted as lack of motivation, loyalty, or dedication. Letting someone know that there are pressing personal issues that must be attended to will help you work out ways to meet the needs of both your job and of your personal life.

Of course, how much you choose to divulge will depend on your relationship with the manager, and we both feel strongly that managers like John, who don't follow through on worries about an employee, really fail—both as compassionate human beings and as managers. When someone is going through a crisis, support is needed from all fronts—including on the job.

EAPs

The EAP, or Employee Assistance Program, is a creature of the 1970s, a time when employers first began to address the individual and organizational costs of alcohol and other drug abuse through performance-based interventions. Through the '70s and into the 1980s, as health benefits cost containment initiatives grew in importance, EAPs grew in sophistication and in the range of crises they "covered."

Today, EAPs take a variety of forms, use a range of assistance models, and generally follow standards set by a professional accreditation organization, the Employee Assistance

Society of North America, with the Employee Assistance Professional Association certifying the qualifications of practitioners.

Costs vary, but a rule of thumb for the cost-benefit analysis in 1995 dollars probably still works *as a ratio* today. Back then, it was estimated that the average annual cost of EAP services per employee ranged from $22 to $28, while the cost of recruiting and training a replacement was estimated at $50,000. Move that ratio to today's dollar equivalents, and you get a good idea of why employers invest in EAPs.

Source: http://www.health.org/workplace/fedagencies/employee_assistance _programs.aspx

SUMMARY

When a life crisis or personal issue threatens to send you to the side of the career highway for an "emergency" stop, consider the following:

1. Assess how you deal with crises.
2. Anticipate potential crises and how they will impact the demands of your career.
3. Prioritize those issues most likely to occur and essential to address.
4. Seek support internally and externally—don't do it alone.

Give Back to the Community:
Expand Yourself as a Person

Janice: It's important to take care of the highway you're driving on, as well as the car. You ride better and more smoothly when the road is well maintained. And that means giving something back to your community or to the world at large.

Bill: Absolutely. If each of us just tends to our own vehicle, the overall highway goes to pot. Adopting a highway keeps us in touch with reality. We do, after all, have a larger responsibility to society.

Janice: And in carrying out that responsibility, we actually do something beneficial for our careers. When the world is out of sync, so is the job. When we do something to try to put the world back in sync, our professional life blossoms as well.

GIVING BACK

Richard was in many ways an exceptional executive—detail oriented, focused, extremely motivated. But he was also myopic: there seemed to be nothing in his life but the task at hand. To execute the task, he burned himself out and drove his staff almost as mercilessly as he drove himself. Senior management appreciated his extraordinary contributions, but they also feared he would crash at some point—and be of no use to himself or anyone else. Their solution was to assign Richard to do volunteer work for the local YMCA.

He was stunned by the assignment, but like the good soldier he was, Richard did as he was ordered and signed up to teach business skills to underprivileged kids two nights a week. The experience was an eye-opener. Until then, Richard had no firsthand knowledge of the difficult circumstances in which some people in his own city lived. He was also astonished by the innate talent and intelligence of many of the young people in his evening class. Teaching these kids something he knew so well tapped into a sensitivity deep within himself; he learned to reach out to others—and to give freely and lovingly.

> **FAST FACT**
>
> In 2002, corporate giving nationwide was $12 billion in cash and in-kind donations, yet individual contributions that year were nearly $184 billion, and individual giving continues to account for more than 76 percent of all charitable giving. Bottom-line? Charities depend on individuals more than on corporations.[1]

Two things happened as a result: Richard enjoyed the most rewarding experience of his life, and he became a much better manager.

That is what will happen when you adopt a highway and take action to give something back to the wider world in which we all live. You will be inwardly rewarded, *and* your career will benefit.

How will doing something not connected to work benefit your

work? Reaching out to others—attending to the road you drive on as well as to your own journey on the road—is one of the best ways there is of expanding your network of contacts. You cannot help but learn something new when you undertake a new initiative outside your normal line of work, and any time you learn something new and stretch your vision, you also open your eyes to other ways you can add value.

Help yourself and your career by helping others: it's a win-win situation you dare not miss. This chapter tells you how to make sure you don't.

WHAT CAN YOU GIVE TO?

When we say giving, we are not talking about money, although by all means, we hope you will write a generous check to a cause or organization you care about. But money is not the point; action is the point, and your actions should spring from passion.

TASK 1: LIST THE AREAS THAT INTEREST YOU; CONNECT THROUGH PASSION

What do you care about? Kids? The elderly? The environment? Affordable housing? There is an issue somewhere at the core of your life. Only you know what it is, but whatever it is, it's your starting point for becoming involved in the wider world.

So right now, sit down and make a list. Remember how angry you became the other day at the litter along the side of the road? Or what about that story in the paper about the working family that made too much money to apply for Medicaid, but not enough to be able to pay for a sick child's medical care? What upsets you in life? Alternatively, what makes your heart soar? Probe your anger and your enthusiasms to find what ignites you.

Task 2: Find Local Service Organizations or Initiatives That Can Respond to Your Passion or Interest

Now that you know what you're interested in doing—the fight you want to fight or the cause you want to further—check out the organization or group or resource that will let you do it. Start locally—check out the Internet or the yellow pages—to find out what's available in your town, city, or neighborhood. Then get on the phone or get on down there and find out how you can help.

On the Internet, type in the keyword that best expresses your interest—"at-risk kids" or "endangered species" or "autism"—and see what you come up with. Call the national organizations you find and ask about local chapters or activities, or plug into action right on the Web site. The Web sites of most volunteer organizations these days enable you to match your interests to their services on both the national and local levels.

Finally, don't forget the old-fashioned ways to find options: check with friends, neighbors, your church, and, of course, your company. Chances are that some people you know are actively involved in local community organizations or charity work—even if they don't talk about it much. Local clergy should certainly be plugged into ways you can help change things in your own backyard. And most companies these days have full-scale departments of corporate philanthropy or corporate citizenship that coordinate the volunteer efforts of employees, point employees in the right direction to meet their charitable interests, and even offer resources to charitable or philanthropic initiatives in which their employees are involved. In short, don't underestimate the power of your own organization.

Here's a template to help you lay it all out:

Focus of Charity	Specific Ones in My Area	My Interest Level (1 low–5 High)	Who I Know on the Board of Directors
Medical Area			
Children			
The Elderly			
The Poor			
Housing			
International			
Other			

TASK 3: HAVE A TRYOUT: ATTEND AN EVENT OR VISIT THE LOCAL ORGANIZATION

Once you have identified one or more of your local options, give them a tryout. At the same time, of course, you may find that you yourself are auditioning for a role in the organization.

Your aim is to see what kinds of activities the organization carries out—and to meet the people involved. Do the activities seem worthwhile to you? Well run? Effective? If not, could you help make them so? Are the people agreeable? Could you see yourself working with them? Do they seem to be doing a good job? Bottom line: Does this organization do work you want to do— and can you add value to the doing of it?

One more thing: Take the family to the event. Maybe it's a sponsored fund-raising race or a field day or a concert. Your own involvement in a local community organization can be greatly enriched if your family joins you in it—and your family can be enriched as well.

WHAT CAN YOU GIVE?

Hal relocated from New York to the Northwest to take a huge job as president of a division of the holding company. The division was based in a large urban center, where the company took its corporate citizenship role very, very seriously. In fact, it was made clear to Hal from the get-go that he needed to "get involved."

He didn't even know where to begin, but a colleague told him about a local organization that served as a shelter and action agency for young girls who had been physically and sexually abused. One of the board members Hal knew quickly took Hal in to learn more about the organization—with a view to Hal's serving on the board.

At first, he thought he wouldn't be able to do it. He simply couldn't bear seeing these little girls—ten years old, twelve years old—who had been abused by adults, often by the very adults who had custody of them. While he has never grown used to the situation, he has learned to deal with it by taking a hand in the care of the girls. It has become a passion, and the passion has fueled only good. Says Hal: "I have learned so much about myself, I feel so connected now to the community, and best of all, I know I can bring value to this organization, which can help these girls turn their young lives around."

> Why not put the effort forth; why not give back to your community?
>
> —MIKE JOHNSON, HOCKEY PLAYER, TORONTO MAPLE LEAFS

Doesn't Hal's involvement seem awfully worthwhile?

You have more to give than you know.

In fact, if your philanthropy up to this point has consisted only of check writing, you're guilty of a failure of imagination and a lack of self-knowledge.

Service organizations need an untold number and variety of functions performed—from stuffing envelopes and painting the headquarters to creating a strategic plan and producing a fund-raising concert. Your training and experience as a manager may suit you to offer the kinds of expertise such organizations too often do not have and very much need—skills in planning, budgeting, marketing, and the like. Certainly, any number of organizations will be happy to take advantage of such know-how—and will be grateful for it.

> Hard work spotlights the character of people: some turn up their sleeves, some turn up their noses, and some don't turn up at all.
>
> —SAM EWING, HUMORIST

By the same token, however, your training and experience should not blind you to the importance of picking up a paintbrush or stuffing an envelope. For the fact is that you give best when you give what is needed. You may have specialized skills to offer; you certainly have a pair of hands and a willing heart. Give what is asked for; even if it's not what you had in mind, you'll be surprised what it will do for you.

GETTING ON BOARDS

One of the best ways to get on board when you set out to adopt your portion of highway is, literally, to get on the board of directors of the organization you want to work with. In such a position, of course, you have a say in policy and a hand in setting strategic vision, goals, and objectives. But as with boards of corporations, getting a seat isn't always easy.

Task 4: Investigate Whether You'll "Fit"—and Can Add Value—on the Board of a Service Organization; If So, Try for a Seat

Your first move should be to see who's on the board. That will give you an idea of what the organization is looking for in a board of directors and whether or not you fit the profile. Are the board members simply well-heeled citizens known for their donations? That's a clue that the organization seeks financial resources—or perhaps serious fund-raising skills.

Or does the makeup of the board indicate that it's more of an advisory panel, made up of far-flung members with little direct impact on day-to-day operations? By contrast, maybe it's a task-force kind of board, with everybody expected to devote real time and effort fulfilling specified work assignments.

> Never doubt that a small group of thoughtful, committed citizens can change the world. Indeed, it is the only thing that ever has.
>
> —Margaret Mead, 1901–1978

Once you know what the organization is looking for in a board member, you have two choices. One, you can present yourself as exactly what they have in mind. Or, two, you can offer them something entirely different as an enhancement to the current board. To a board made up solely of wealthy people, offer to raise funds from new sources. To a board composed of "remote presences," present yourself as a concerned local citizen who will add a community and neighborhood value to the expertise of all those outsiders.

The key is to fulfill a need the board is lacking. As an example, suppose the charity has a major expansion plan. Are you in the construction or real estate business? Do you have risk management expertise? Those are two business skills that would probably bring real value to a board in that situation. The key is to identify what your favorite charity needs. We've provided a chart that will help you do that.

YOUR VALUE TO A BOARD

Names of Charities	Their Needs	Value You Bring

We don't give many guarantees in this book, but we guarantee you this: whatever the portion of highway you adopt, wherever it is, whatever you do to maintain it, you'll get back far more than you give.

SUMMARY

Your drive down the career highway will be smoother, faster, and far more rewarding if you pay attention to the road itself and extend a helping hand to maintain it. Here's how to get involved:

1. List the areas that interest you; connect through passion.
2. Find service organizations or initiatives available locally that "fit" with your passion or interest.
3. Have a tryout: attend an event or visit the local organization.
4. Investigate whether you'll "fit"—and can add value—on the board of a service organization. If so, try for a seat.

Cracking the Corporate Code:
Learn the Language of Success

Bill: Like learning a foreign language if you move to another country, it is critical to learn the company jargon. In Paris, you'd better know the difference between *allez* and *arretez,* or you'll be cruising for a crash.

Janice: That's true; it's essential to master the corporate language, not just of the job but of your company's culture and style. You simply have to learn to read the signals.

Bill: Absolutely. If the name of the corporate game is "teamwork," and you work in the "I" mode, you could be in big trouble.

Janice: And it's not enough to be able to understand the obvious; you also have to crack the unwritten code. I'm talking about the unspoken rules of the road, where there are no road signs.

Bill: For the newcomer, there are potholes everywhere. And you can be sure the rules of the road from your last job or your last company won't totally apply in your new place.

PARLEZ-VOUS JARGON?

Mark Anderson arrived at his new job bright eyed and bushy tailed, enthusiastic about the company and eager to make a difference in it. On Day One of the job, his boss assigned him three tasks:

1. Analyze the decrease in the rate of heads booked over the past three quarters.
2. Assess the benefits of introducing TQM into the digitizing process.
3. Research a best-of-breed integration solution for our treeware problem.

Mark didn't understand a word. Some of what he didn't get was, he felt certain, technical terminology—jargon of the job, stuff he figured they expected him to know. But some of it was surely company jargon—terms that meant something very specific in this company and something else entirely everywhere else.

Naturally, Mark did not want to appear to be ignorant—not on the first day of the job. He certainly did not want to bother the boss with dumb questions like, "What do you mean by this?" That, he was certain, was a fast road to the kind of impression he did not want to make. But *TQM? Heads booked? Treeware?* These were like road signs in a foreign language: miss their meaning, and you could go the wrong way, hit something hard, or worst of all, get pulled over and given a summons. Not a good way to start a new job. What he needed, Mark decided, was an interpreter—someone who could translate the language for him, teach him the basics.

There were a couple of guys standing at the entrances to their cubicles talking, so Mark headed down the hall toward them, but as he approached, he heard one say to the other, "It was salmon day for me, man. I got totally betamaxed by Louise's proposal. I tried for a groin pull, just to regain control of the meeting, but frankly, I blew my buffer, and that was it." What the guy *really* meant was that after swimming upstream all day, he had lost in the end anyway. He was totally overtaken by Louise's inferior but better-marketed proposal. He had then *tried* to intimidate his colleagues with his overwhelming machismo, but he had lost his train of thought midstream. Yeah, that's what he meant . . . but Mark didn't get it.

So he kept walking. This was going to be tougher than he thought. He wasn't just in a new job; he might as well be in a new country, driving a strange car, with right-hand drive and the traffic in the left lane and the road signs absolutely incomprehensible . . .

BUSINESS BERLITZ

You wouldn't travel to a foreign country without a phrase book for the language along with your guidebook and maps, and you certainly wouldn't drive a foreign road without a cheat sheet for what the signs say. And you would not get behind the wheel of a foreign car with the steering wheel on the "wrong" side without getting instructions or reading the manual. Ditto for entering the foreign territory of a new job or new company.

It's simple: corporations run on the fuel of common language. Think about it. From the chairman's annual end-of-year speech, to the confidential e-mail explaining why sales plummeted last month, to the directive to frontline workers about a new procedure for customer service, nothing gets done unless it's communicated, and communication happens through language.

Jargon is a special dialect of language, whether it's the jargon of a particular kind of job or a specific corporate culture. Doctors have a jargon, and so do baseball players—much of it in sign language—and so do corporate managers. What's more, doctors in a specific hospital develop their own jargon—especially during surgery, when they need to communicate fast. Players on different baseball teams and the employees in different corporations do the same: come up with their own set of buzzwords that derive organically from the particular organization's culture and purpose and that serve as shortcuts of understanding for those in the know.

> When you travel, remember that a foreign country is not designed to make you comfortable. It is designed to make its own people comfortable.
>
> —CLIFTON FADIMAN, WRITER/CRITIC

But jargon also freezes out those not in the know. It froze out Mark Anderson, feeling hapless and isolated five minutes into his new job, as lost as an English-speaking traveler in Europe who doesn't know what *Sortie* (French for "exit") and *Eintritt* (German for "entrance") mean—and therefore not knowing whether he's coming or going. In business, however, language fluency requires more than just knowing whether you're coming or going. In fact, cracking the code of your organization is the essential foundation for doing your job at all, much less for succeeding.

TASK 1: KNOW THE JOB'S JARGON—AND WHAT'S EXPECTED OF YOU

Nothing is worse than the situation in which Mark Anderson found himself on the first day of his new job: clueless as to what was being asked of him. There's little excuse these days not to know that TQM is Total Quality Management or that booking heads means eliminating jobs or that treeware refers to manuals and hard copies. But there's every reason to ask questions about the application of TQM in the organization, about how head count is measured, and about exactly what constitutes the treeware *problem*.

Mark should have asked. Yes, it was up to his boss to be clear about his instructions, but by being afraid or unwilling to ask for elucidation, Mark simply compounded the boss's failure and pretty much ensured his own. Looking "dumb," as Mark feared, is not nearly as costly as failing to do the job you've been assigned. Besides, asking key questions doesn't make you look dumb; it makes you look determined to get things right. And the most appropriate time to ask what may seem like "dumb" questions is early on. If you wait too long, you look dumb for not knowing the obvious.

It is not essential or even always right to put questions to the boss. There are plenty of resources providing technical information on such topics as TQM; all you need to do is search on a keyword. As for company-specific knowledge, Mark could have asked the boss one simple question about his three-task assignment: "Where do I go—what's my resource or whom do I ask—for information on these tasks?" He could easily have added, "I admit these tasks are new for me, and I want to be absolutely sure I understand your expectations."

Bottom line? The best way to find out the essentials for doing your job is to ask; learning the language of the job is up to you.

DRIVING TIP: JOB JARGON AND TECHNICAL LINGO

Glossaries abound on the Internet. To find one that can help you figure out your job's jargon or to learn the technical terms of an assignment, just do a search on [SUBJECT MATTER] GLOSSARY, and see what you come up with. For example, try searching on FINANCIAL GLOSSARY, TQM GLOSSARY, SIX SIGMA

GLOSSARY, PROJECT MANAGEMENT GLOSSARY, and the like. Bookmark the glossary or glossaries you need, and print out key terms to keep handy—just like the Basics page of a foreign language phrase book. And while you're online, read all the public information on or about your new company; much of what you need to know could well be explained right there.

TASK 2: LEARN YOUR ORGANIZATION'S OPERATING LANGUAGE

When we speak about an organization's "operating language," we mean the unwritten rules about the way things are done and about how the place really works. For the new hire, the key here is to make your mind a blank slate. Don't assume that the way things worked on your last job or in your former company is the way things are going to work here. In fact, assume the opposite; that way at least you'll be able to observe objectively. (And please, please never say, "In my old job we did it this way." It's a killer.)

The way things work includes whether or not people arrive in the office early. Do they stay late? Take long or short lunches? Are cubicles cluttered with family photos, or are they sparely furnished and minimally decorated? What about e-mailing, Internet usage, cell phones, and taking care of personal business on company time?

Some organizations like written procedures to be followed to the letter; in others, procedures are just so much treeware. Some companies have a system for everything, and woe betide the staffer who tries to buck the system. Other organizations don't care what process you use—as long as you achieve the objective.

In any new assignment or new job, take your time early on to ask questions and defer to others. Of course, you want to hit the ground running, but you want to be running in the right direction, on the right road, and for the right reasons. And you want to be able to read the signs while going 75 mph.

Task 3: Sync Your Style to the Situation

HP was a quintessentially "California" kind of company, one that managed to be both brilliantly innovative and pleasantly laid-back at the same time. It was every egghead's favorite company, and while it was always fiercely and proudly competitive, it also seemed to wear the "natural" label—the organic food among all that processed junk.

Carly Fiorina, by contrast, was the quintessential 1990s slash-and-burn executive. Brought in to shake up the lumbering company and leapfrog it into the Internet era, Fiorina made big changes fast—and came to a crashing halt as a result.

It probably wasn't what she did that lost her the confidence of the board, but rather the way she did it. The truth is that the way she did it may have been the only way it was going to get done; nevertheless, it was out of sync with HP's style, and Fiorina took the hit.

So did John Mack, the legendary Wall Street deal maker hired by Credit Suisse First Boston in 2001, precisely to shake up the troubled Swiss institution and put it back on its feet. Three years later, the press reported that Mack the Knife got stabbed in the back by the top brass in Zurich, to whom he had become more pain-in-the-neck than savior. The immediate reason for Mack's ouster was his failure to persuade the board to pursue a merger with another European financial behemoth, but the underlying cause was more profound. "He's not Swiss," one analyst said, and while the Zurich-based board of directors thought it wanted a hotshot American in charge, when push came to shove, the Wall Street style was not to their liking.

Nor was the passivity exhibited by the gnomes of Zurich what

Mack was used to. His relentlessly competitive, score-keeping style worked better on Wall Street, and that's where you'll find him today, stylistically comfortable and at home since 2005 as chairman and CEO of Morgan Stanley.

Style is very much part of the language of a company, and style clashes can be brutally destructive. That's why it's essential to read the style of your new organization and get in sync with it as soon as possible.

This is not a question of personal style; your personal style is something you bring with you always, wherever you go. What we mean here is the distinctive idiom of the organization—the behavior and customs that are peculiar to it and to no place else. Is the company run by consensus, consultation, dictatorship, or democracy—as you observed back at Road Sign 6? However it is run stylistically, clash with the style as a newbie in the organization —especially as an executive—and you could be en route to an early smashup on this career highway.

So take a moment to reflect on the style of the organization you're in—and assess how well you understand the stylistic code.

CRACK THE CODE—STYLISTICALLY

Language/jargon unique to the organization	
What am I unfamiliar with?	
How do I get comfortable with jargon?	
Where and when do I demonstrate my knowledge of jargon?	

We've seen instance after instance where a stylistic disconnect between a new executive and the company has been deadly—with lots of accidental tourists getting smashed in the pileup. That's why it's so important that when you're new to a place, you learn to translate the signs at every level and in every encounter—with your boss or other superiors, with subordinates, with those who lost out on the opportunity you got, with any subsidiary you may be working with, and with such external constituents as clients, analysts, and competitors. With each, you must know exactly what your mandate is.

For example, if your boss hired you to be a "change agent" and turn things around, you need to know what that means—and you need to ask if your assumption of the role has been communicated to the troops. If not, nothing you say or do will be understood. If it has been communicated, what do you need to know to operate in such a way that the changes happen? With whom should you be consulting? How does it work? How do you get input in this place? How do you get buy-in? All are aspects of style. Go against the style in any of the key ways—or misunderstand the style, or worse, spurn the style—and you're setting yourself up for failure.

Here's a chart to help you block out an approach:

Mandates: What Is Expected of Me, and By Whom?	Stylistically, How Do I Execute and with Whom Do I Communicate?
1.	1.
2.	2.
3.	3.

Maybe you're used to a consultative style, and the style in your new organization is distinctly monarchical. That means that all your efforts to consult with a range of stakeholders seem like just so much brownnosing. Or maybe you have come from a top-down hierarchy to a matrix organization—and right off the bat, you've failed to communicate with your multiple bosses. That's a bad start. Or maybe your responses to your new environment are seen as emotionally off-key, and you've been labeled from the very beginning as someone who doesn't fit in with the organization. Any one of these scenarios can at best burden and at worst doom your efforts to succeed on the job.

The bottom line, therefore, is to understand the spoken, unspoken, and style codes through close observation of how others have operated successfully. Unless you are the CEO and the board of directors all in one, assume that the organization will not bend to fit you. Break the code, or the one who breaks will most likely be you.

SUMMARY

When you can't read the signs on the highway or understand the directions you're given, pull over and take some language lessons:

1. Know the job's jargon—and what's expected of you.
2. Learn your organization's operating language.
3. Sync your style to the situation.

Don't Be Held Back by Gender, Race, Pedigree: Learn How to Get Invited to the Party

Janice: In your coaching, do you get a sense from the women and minorities you work with that they feel their career options are limited? Or do they believe they're in demand as companies seek diversity?

Bill: Both. There's often a sense of insecurity about how they arrived at the job—and a sense of resentment that their opportunities are limited. Many feel—rightly—that they have been asked to the party, but only to sit there and look pretty, not to say anything.

Janice: Does a corporate snobbery still exist about background, elite colleges, other affiliations?

Bill: Yes.

Janice: I see that as well. I think pedigree and education are still issues. And those who did not graduate from top-tier schools *and* who are women or minorities get a double dose of that kind of elitist rejection.

THE OPPORTUNITY DOOR:
OPEN, CLOSED, OR AJAR?

Brilliant, handsome, holder of two degrees from *the* top-tier university, involved in the community, fantastic with people—his boss said that "his ability to read a group is amazing"—and an extraordinary asset to the corporation, Richard had absolutely everything going for him. True, he had quietly suspected that his race—Richard is African-American—may have opened the corporate door for him, but he also knew that he had pushed the envelope in the company, hitting home run after home run year after year. Still, with ten years of superior performance under his belt, Richard worried that the top doors in the company were nevertheless closed to him because of who he was, not what he did and how well he did it.

When a clearly inferior performer was promoted ahead of him, Richard protested.

"It's because you're not a team player," he was told.

"This is the first I've heard of it," Richard replied.

"Well," company management responded, "we'll send you for some coaching."

In his first meeting with Bill, Richard was asked to assess honestly whether the company, despite all of his achievements, had placed a Do Not Enter sign on the fast track for minorities. If so, Bill suggested, Richard's only options were to change his modus operandi, move on to another corporation, or possibly seek legal recourse.

Let's be honest: for some people, in some industries and in some companies, there is a Do Not Enter sign on the career highway. It closes off access to the most rewarding part of the drive: the view from the very top of the hill. It is aimed at those with whom the folks who run things don't feel comfortable. They don't feel comfortable with them because they don't know them, and they don't know them because they put up the Do Not Enter signs to keep them out. This vicious circle excludes women and minorities, to be sure, but it also excludes those who did not go to the right schools, who did not belong to the right fraternities, or do not play golf at the right clubs.

By the same token, we must with equal honesty affirm that corporate hiring and professional development today emphasize diversity. In an increasingly global market, where companies need to "look like" their customers, diversity is good business. It is also good business in an increasingly competitive market, where every talent is needed and every individual's potential must therefore be realized.

Women, minorities, and others who don't quite belong to "the old-boy network" thus can find themselves hung up on the horns of a dilemma: their "diversity" may give them an initial advantage, but it may also keep them from being able to fully exploit the advantage.

> I have not been animated in my life to fight against race and sex discrimination simply because of my own identity. That would mean that one must be South African to fight apartheid, or a poor white in Appalachia to fight poverty, or Jewish to fight anti-Semitism. And I just reject that conception of how struggles should be waged.
>
> —ELEANOR HOLMES NORTON, U.S. REPRESENTATIVE, DISTRICT OF COLUMBIA

They're offered a nice car to drive the career highway, but there are only a few gallons of gas in the tank—not enough to make it to the top of the hill. We have no problem stating categorically that we think this is wrong and foolish. Unfortunately, it is also a fact of life that must be reckoned with and dealt with.

TASK 1: FIND OUT IF THERE IS A DO NOT ENTER SIGN ON YOUR CAREER HIGHWAY

The first task is to assess candidly and carefully if you're being deliberately kept away from the top of that hill. To do that, you must take a hard look at your own performance in the context of the performance of others—men, nonminority members, and those whose pedigrees mark them as belonging to the same "tribe" as the company's senior managers and culture shapers.

Use this chart to help you track where your performance has taken you versus where the similar performance of those others has taken them. How are you doing relative to men, if you're female; to nonminorities, if you're a minority; and, whether you are man, woman, or minority, relative to those with better pedigrees? If there's a disparity in favor of white males who wear the right tie, that's a hint that you may be seeing a Do Not Enter sign up ahead.

DO-NOT-ENTER INDICATOR CHART

Progress Indicator	You	Men	Nonminority	Pedigree (Social Status, Schools, Family Name)
Pay				
Perks				
Promotions				
Choice Assumptions				
Title				
Special Project Task Forces				

Progress Indicator	You	Men	Nonminority	Pedigree (Social Status, Schools, Family Name)
Informal Time with the Leader				
Office Location				
Support Staff				
Other				

Also, of course, check out the numbers of people from your "tribe"—women, minorities, etc.—who have been appointed to senior positions. Are their jobs substantial assignments in terms of budget and staff—or are they "soft" assignments, with little impact, direct or indirect, on the bottom line? If the latter, it's a hint that "diversity" is honored more in theory than in practice, and it's a sign that you, too, may be able to rise no higher than window dressing.

There is no doubt that with regard to both women and minorities, progress is being made. But it is painfully slow. In her book *Why So Slow?*, Professor Virginia Valian of Hunter College in New York investigates a number of factors that have thwarted the advancement of women. Here are a few:

1. The minimal comfort men feel with women because of the socialization process when they were young boys, which basically excluded girls
2. The fact that most of men's associations with women outside of the workplace have been with people who looked after them—mothers, wives, etc.

3. Men's reluctance to give up their positions of power to anyone—especially a woman

Read Professor Valian's book to get a better idea of all this, but we also suggest you read our book *What Every Successful Woman Knows* for ideas on how to break through the glass ceilings and knock down the iron walls.

TASK 2: IF YOU SEE OR SUSPECT A DO NOT ENTER SIGN, START BUILDING BRIDGES

The bridges need to be both internal and external. You want to build internal bridges as a way to start moving *over*. Lateral moves broaden your résumé, hedge your bets against downsizing, and can be good preparation for moving out. For Richard at the start of this chapter, building internal bridges meant changing his modus operandi to become the "team player" he had not been seen to be. In other words, building internal bridges meant changing perceptions.

> At the current rate at which women are being added to boards of directors, it will take another 70 years before parity is reached within the Fortune 500 ranks.[1]

As for external bridges, they serve, quite simply, as a way out—and you want to start building them well before that Do Not Enter sign raises its ugly head.

Start by drawing two circles, one inside the other. Put yourself at the dead center of the circles; then start filling the circles with the names of people who could conceivably connect you to another position, department, division, or company—or could help you move over or out in some way. The inner circle should be filled with the names of people who can help you internally;

the outer circle is for those who might connect you to other organizations.

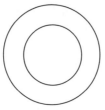

To assist your internal bridge builders in helping you, you will need an action plan. The plan should focus on your doing three things in particular:

- Demonstrating a unique ability to your current boss
- Identifying the value you can add to your organization in other divisions
- Articulating the skills you have and will develop to meet the company's changing needs

Plot your action plan here:

	Action Step 1	Action Step 2	Action Step 3	Action Step 4
Make Myself More Valuable to My Boss				
Value to Other Divisions; How to Transfer the Opportunity				
Skills Needed for Future				

To start building external bridges, make a list of where those external bridge builders might take you—that is, determine what function or responsibility each of them has, and figure out how each might connect you elsewhere. Then determine what skills you would need once the connection is made, and devise an action plan for acquiring those needed skills. Assume you will need as many skills as possible for your next career move.

Another important tool for building the external network is the work you did at Road Sign 14—getting involved in the activities or on the boards of civic and/or charitable organizations. These can offer strong connections to other people and other organizations—connections you can call on to help you when a Do Not Enter sign appears on your career highway.

SUMMARY

If there's a Do Not Enter sign up ahead for your career, take steps now to find another road:

1. Find out if there is a Do Not Enter sign on your career highway.
2. If you see or suspect a Do Not Enter sign, start building bridges internally and externally.

Ethics and You: How *Not* to Compromise Your Values or Tarnish Your Reputation

Bill: Are candidates concerned about company executives being in the press regarding corporate governance issues and inappropriate behaviors?

Janice: People are concerned about what that will mean regarding their long-term careers, although some see it as an opportunity for them to bring order to chaos and an end to corruption.

Bill: And the executive compensation issue has certainly raised the eyebrows of employers and shareholders. The *Financial Times* reported that from 1991 to 2001, the CEOs involved in the twenty-five largest business collapses walked away with $3.3 billion in personal compensation: so much for "pay for performance."

Janice: Exactly. It's no wonder trust in top management is at an all-time low—from leaders who failed to lead to those who were corrupt. Yes, they all got big bucks, but a lot also went to prison.

Bill: Candidates and current employers have to be concerned that they don't drive onto the soft shoulder and ruin their careers. How to do that is key to one's reputation.

THE THING THAT MONEY CAN'T BUY

Jeffrey Wigand from Brown & Williamson. Coleen Rowley of the FBI. Sherron Watkins from Enron. These are today's corporate heroes—whistle-blowers, every one. They pointed out the financial malfeasance, cronyism, incompetence, and outright lying of corporate leadership. It is they who should gain our admiration and thanks, not the razzle-dazzle CEOs who flare up like meteors, only to land, all too often, in legal trouble. For the crimes and misdemeanors of a few bad apples, today's corporate professional is basically guilty till proven innocent when it comes to core ethical values.

> You cannot have a proud and chivalrous spirit if your conduct is mean and paltry; for whatever a man's actions are, such must be his spirit.
>
> —DEMOSTHENES, 384–322 BC

This is the soft shoulder of corporate life today, and it can be a hard place to drive your career car. We're talking here about standards of behavior that govern not just how we do business, but also how we conduct ourselves every day on the job—in our dealings with subordinates, peers, and superiors; in providing value for the money we are paid; in carrying out our responsibilities to ourselves and to our principles. We are talking, in short, about the shadow land of ethics and integrity—for both ourselves and the establishments we work for.

It is a shadow land because the rules are not always clear, because standards may differ from one organization to another and from individual to individual, because in the end, it's your own moral compass that must drive you. The danger is that you may let it drive you onto the soft shoulder. And if you've ever driven on one, you know what a soft shoulder is like: it's like being stuck in snow or mired in mud or sinking in quicksand. You can power up the engine as much as you want, rock back and forth till the motor overheats, but the truth is, you're stuck, and you can't get out.

YOUR PERSONAL ETHICS

Of course, there are laws that must be followed, and with corporate governance in the harsh spotlight of suspicious surveillance these days, those laws—like the Sarbanes-Oxley Act of 2002—must be complied with to the letter. That is a clear road sign, but road signs alone do not cover all the territory of ethical behavior. Good judgment also must prevail.

To the corporate professional on a daily basis, your own set of individual values is most pertinent. The burden of working in a culture whose values are out of sync with your own can be oppressive. Some bend under the weight—and often regret it later. Some just break. Others leave the job or the company or the industry or corporate life altogether.

At the start of a career, we are all so eager for advancement, for big bucks, for the thrill of doing well and rising higher. Happy to be driving in that fast lane, we sometimes tend to look the other way if we see things that don't seem right to us, or we rationalize our way out of our own ethical dilemmas, or we tell ourselves that this is how the game is played. It is always, always a mistake to do so.

For one thing, avoidance of ethical actions or indifference to the values you believe in eventually erodes the very core of who you are. We have personally seen the results of that kind of erosion time and again—in executives who would give back the stock options in a minute if they could regain the respect of others.

Others we've seen wish they could exchange the time they've spent in power grabbing for time with their children. Still others know they lost the most important thing in the world when they told themselves that their promotion was more important than the coworker who was being mistreated, or that "this is just the way things work." Things don't just work that way, and if you let them, you run the risk of losing your self-respect, dignity, and reputation.

There is also a very practical reason why you must honor ethical values every day: not honoring them can come back to bite you later on. Your reputation is like your skin: you can't shake it; it goes where you go. Once you're labeled, it's almost impossible to get unlabeled. Anyone who has ever earned a bad reputation—as a sleaze, or as someone willing to support a sleaze, or as one who can be counted on to look the other way and keep mum—knows it is virtually impossible to change that perception and rebuild a reputation as someone trustworthy. Fortunately or unfortunately, perception is all in this case.

Yes, it's hard to think about the long road when you're confronted by a short-term dilemma; the end of the long road can seem very far away indeed. But a long road is precisely what a career is. It really isn't speed that counts; it's getting where you want to go. If you have to slow down now to keep your career on the straight path and avoid the soft shoulder, it is well worth it. Do we sound a little preachy? We are sure we do. But listen up. This discussion is critical.

THE ETHICAL CORPORATION

Is the "ethical corporation" a contradiction in terms? Some people think so, and recent history gives their claim some support. For a while there, in the early part of the twenty-first century, corporate America seemed to epitomize highly *un*ethical behavior, with often tragic consequences. Enron, Tyco, WorldComm, Adelphia: the names read like a rogues' gallery of greed, excess, cheating, and downright theft. Yet it's probably fair to say that every one of these companies had a "statement of values" embossed in some glossy brochure or repeated regularly in its annual reports. The problem was that the bosses seemed to think those values did not apply to them.

What's the impact of such indifference on the managers and professionals who make up the bulk of the companies' workforce? At Enron, for example, whether some of the rank and file knew of unethical behavior and "went along" or had no idea and just did their

> It is curious that physical courage should be so common in the world and moral courage so rare.
>
> —MARK TWAIN, 1835–1910

work every day, the consequences were alarmingly similar: loss. Life-changing loss of their retirement pensions, of assets they relied on, of their livelihoods, of their future. It's a steep price to pay for working in a company where the reality was light-years away from the rhetoric.

So blinding have been the headlines about the likes of Enron that we forget that most companies and CEOs are honorable. What's more, the serious problems that beset much of corporate America in the wake of the Enron-Tyco-WorldComm-Adelphia scandals—the insensitivity at the top, the indifference to corruption—also present an opportunity for new thinking and behaviors.

And there are signs that many companies and their corporate

> Prefer loss to the wealth of dishonest gain; the former vexes you for a time; the latter will bring you lasting remorse.
>
> —Chilo

leaders are seizing the opportunity. Look at Proctor & Gamble, for example, where chairman/CEO A. G. Lafley has fostered an environment in which employees pool their brainpower and experience to nurture a whole new kind of organization, with a whole new kind of dynamic. The P&G pattern suggests a model for successful CEOs in the twenty-first century: they will have to set high standards for their organizations and scrupulously observe those standards themselves. Indeed, the future will belong to those executives who come down off their lofty perches, set tough but fair standards for themselves and their organization, and make their first priority the unleashing of the creative potential of their own people. That's what we would call an *ethical* corporation.

Does it sound like a place where you would be happy working? We bet it does.

Task 1: Get Clarity on Your Company's Corporate Values

That's why the first task for avoiding the soft ethical shoulder in your career is to be absolutely clear about the core values your company espouses. And companies espouse values almost as a routine matter these days. "Our Values" statements appear in orientation kits, company brochures, even incised into the wall of the building's lobby. And so they should, for a corporation's values are the standards it claims to live by, and everyone should know precisely what those values are. So Task 1 is to get hold of the official corporate statement on values and to make sure you understand it.

How many others understand it? Is the "values list" widely disseminated—or is it an afterthought? Is it paid lip service—or emphasized routinely by corporate leadership? Put it this way: What significance does the statement of values have in your company?

What should these values cover? That is to say, what makes a corporation ethical? Expressed commitments to product quality, customer satisfaction, employee wages and benefits, fairness and respect in personnel matters, transparency and accountability in all functions, and local community and environmental responsibilities are rock-bottom basics. All of these, by the way, are issues that a company can actually influence.

But as we all know, words can obscure as well as illumine. That's why this task isn't just about finding out what the company's values are, but about getting clarity on them—making absolutely certain you understand them. This chart will help you do both:

YOUR COMPANY'S CORPORATE VALUES

Value	Statement of What They Mean
1._____	_____
2._____	_____
3._____	_____
4._____	_____
5._____	_____

ETHICS AND INTEGRITY IN THE CORPORATE WORKPLACE

The American Management Association polled American corporations on the subject of values. Seventy percent of respondents said that their company's corporate values included ethics and integrity high on the list. Seventy-one percent of corporations state their values in employee handbooks, 60 percent list them in company brochures, and 50 percent post them on their corporate Web sites.[1]

Does yours?

TASK 2: DETERMINE: DO THEY MEAN IT?

Talk is cheap. Nothing is easier than putting words down on a piece of paper for all to see. But does this corporation's leadership *really* mean it concerning their values, and if so, how is it evidenced?

A lot of this will be readily visible to the naked eye. If your corporate leadership spouts a lot of talk about the importance of spending time with family, but you notice that the CEO is in the office every weekend and has been divorced four times, that's a pretty good indication that he doesn't really mean it about family values—or worse, that he doesn't think the values the corporation talks about apply to him! That's why it's important to run a reality check on the disconnects, if any, between what corporate leadership says and how it really behaves.

The best way to check that out is to map words and deeds. Here's a chart that will help:

CORPORATE VALUES MAP

Corporate Values	Behaviors of Corporate Management That Show Support for the Value	Behaviors of Corporate Management That Show Lack of Support for the Value

For example, the statement of a corporation's values announces loud and clear that "our employees are our most valuable resource." How does the company show support for that value? What behaviors have you seen that bring that announcement to life?

Judy Johnson worked for a company that listed that very statement as its absolute top value. Yet when she told her boss she was expecting a child in six months, he took her off the team of a major account "as a precaution," he said, in case she "couldn't be there when the big campaign kicked off." But what if a man on the account team were to become ill during the big campaign? Wouldn't the team have had to muddle through somehow? Judy rightly saw this "precautionary"

> Ethical axioms are found and tested not very differently from the axioms of science. Truth is what stands the test of experience.
>
> —ALBERT EINSTEIN, 1879–1955

assumption as evidence that the number one value on the corporate list was honored more in theory than in fact. Check column 3 in the Corporate Values Map for that one: management's behavior doesn't support management's stated value.

On the other hand, the company also says it values "giving back to the community." Judy knows firsthand how true this is. When she headed her community's Help the Homeless drive, the company's community service department swung into high gear, providing logistical help, public relations resources, even some funding. What's more, her bonus was higher precisely because of her involvement in the drive. So score one for the company on that value at least; place a check mark in column 2 and describe precisely how management behaves to demonstrate support of the giving-back-to-the-community value.

CORPORATE ETHICS:
MAKING COMMITMENT COUNT

One of the most dastardly deeds ever to afflict corporate America offers an object lesson in the importance of corporate actions matching corporate public relations. In 1982, someone—the perpetrator has never been caught—laced some bottles of Tylenol capsules with cyanide. Seven people died, and the country as a whole panicked. It's probably fair to say that corporate management at Johnson & Johnson, makers of Tylenol, also panicked, at least initially. The seven deaths instantly killed the company's reputation and that of their leading product, and there seemed no solution.

But there was. In a series of costly remedial actions, J&J recalled 31 million bottles of Tylenol capsules—at a total value of more than $100 million—and offered to exchange any Tylenol capsule products for Tylenol tablets—also at a cost of millions. The company made no disclaimer; it did not suggest that "someone else" was at fault, although someone else was; it did not scurry to excuse itself as a way of saving its reputation. And in this way, it actually enhanced its reputation. In 1982, J&J spent a lot to do the right thing, to honor the value of customer safety first and foremost. Today, as is well known, Tylenol has made a full comeback and leads its market. In every way, Johnson & Johnson's demonstrated commitment to its core values was worth it.

YOUR ETHICAL COMPASS

It didn't take Pete Hamilton long to realize that business travel, which had looked so glamorous when he was in B-school, was actually exhausting, tedious, and not much fun. The only thing that made it bearable to be away from home for a week at a time was the relaxing evening dinner with colleagues and the comforts and occasional luxuries of good hotels. So he was surprised more than anything else when he saw his colleagues routinely abuse their expense accounts, sometimes doubling or even tripling their claims, and often making purchases for personal items that they charged to the corporate credit card. What bothered him almost as much was the way the guys joked about it, making a game of coming up with names of fictitious clients to pad their expense accounts and finding "business reasons" for the personal purchases. "Do this right," one colleague confided with a smile, "and you can pretty much live on the expense account and bank your salary."

So Pete went to see his boss, who just happened to be the deputy to the company's chief financial officer. The boss listened carefully to everything Pete had to say. Then he responded. "Come off it, Hamilton," the deputy CFO said. "These guys are veterans of this company, and it's entirely inappropriate for you to bring this up. If I were you, I wouldn't mention it again. And I'll try to forget that you brought it up at all."

For Pete Hamilton, the cheating he had seen was now compounded by the collusion. With a wink, a nod, and a chastising lecture, his concerns had been summarily dismissed. For Pete, it was too much. Although the job was his first one, and though he had not been with the company for long, it was impossible for him to stay. Even a transfer to a position in a different division held no allure for Pete. He believed he had seen into the core of the company and had found it rotten. He got out.

Perhaps you think Pete's reaction was extreme. Or perhaps you believe there were other steps he should have taken to correct the problem inside the company before he just up and left. Maybe. The point is that Pete Hamilton followed his own ethical compass, not his company's and not anyone else's. He'll sleep well tonight and for the rest of his career—and that counts for a lot.

TASK 3: DECIDE IF YOU CAN LIVE WITH THE ETHICAL DISCONNECTS, IF ANY, IN YOUR WORK SITUATION

How do you know your core values? Task 3 will help you find and articulate them. It's a matter of looking at the gaps, if any, between your corporation's words and its deeds, and then deciding which gaps you can live with and which are simply insupportable.

This is an exercise that will let you know, with crystal clarity, exactly what your values are. It will help you draw the line you simply will not cross. You'll learn what you are prepared to do—and what you are not prepared to do—if your values are compromised at work or if you find that your company's values are out of sync with your own.

First, go back to the Corporate Values Map and take a hard look at those corporate values that are not evidenced in corporate behavior or that are honored only in words, not deeds. Where do you stand on each of these value disconnects? Write down your own feelings about the disconnect; then score how important the value—and its failure in the corporation—is to you. That leaves only one question: What are you going to do about it?

Judy Johnson saw her boss's dismissing her from the account team "preemptively" as a fundamental wrong. She saw it as a violation of the corporate standard about the way employees should be treated, and it clarified her own feelings about fairness, gender discrimination, and equal opportunity. How important was that to this young woman who was soon to be the mother of a daughter? It was of paramount importance. Judy decided she could not sit by and let it happen; it was, in her eyes and for her career, simply insupportable. She worked out a series of actions she was prepared to take to remedy the situation—in her words, "to make the company take its own value statement seriously." Step 1 of Judy's action plan was to reengage her boss, ask him to put her back on the team, and let him know she intended to pursue the matter. This she was prepared to do—as far as a legal challenge, if necessary. It would mean taking some risks and expending a good deal of time, energy, and personal commitment, but Judy had realized that, for her own sake and in her own eyes, she could simply do no less.

> Ethics and equity
> and the principles
> of justice do
> not change with
> the calendar.
>
> —D. H. LAWRENCE,
> BRITISH WRITER,
> 1885–1930

Here's a chart to help you work through Task 3:

Corporate Value Not Practiced	My Value	Importance to Me 1 to 5 (low to high)	Action Plan

---

EXECUTIVE COMPENSATION: THE STOCK-OPTION DEBACLE

How much is too much? That is certainly part of the problem with today's executive compensation packages, at least in the eyes of most Americans. The excesses that were focused on after 2001 struck the bulk of the nation as simply unfair—outsized in terms of the value received for the dollars paid, and unjust in terms of taking dollars out of the pockets of shareholders, many of them working families with retirement savings.

But what really bothered people most was the makeup of many executive compensation packages—specifically, the reliance on stock options, which were seen as an incentive to bad, short-term decision making with no downside risk for the executive making the decisions. Moreover, because stock options did not have to be expensed in company financial statements, a lot of companies began to see them as free money, and this preferential accounting treatment also was perceived as unfair.

With so many strikes against stock options, it's perhaps no wonder that companies are moving away from including them in executive compensation packages, with their use nearly halved in the four-year period from 2001 to 2004.

The bottom line is not about money or other perks you might receive. It is about staying off the soft shoulder. Good ethics starts with you. If you do right from the beginning of your career, avoiding any compromise to your own core values, you will very likely not be stopped by the other road signs in this book. The obvious, however, is not always so obvious—as we have seen. Pay attention to that inner voice, and follow your own moral compass, and at the end of the day, you'll still be driving straight and clear and free along your career highway.

SUMMARY

A career can get permanently hung up in the soft shoulder of fudged ethics and compromised values. To avoid stalling out or getting stuck at the side of the highway, do the following:

1. Get clarity on your company's corporate values.
2. Determine if they mean it.
3. Decide if you can live with the ethical disconnects, if any, in your work situation.

```
TRAFFIC
FINES
DOUBLED
IN
WORK
ZONE
```

The Business of Etiquette:
A Tool for Competitive Advantage

Janice: I don't think people understand how important etiquette is in business.

Bill: Time after time, I've seen really talented people get known for their lack of etiquette instead of for their talents.

Janice: I see the smartest candidates asking the dumbest questions. They seem suited in every way for a position, and then they do or say something totally inappropriate.

Bill: It happens on the job as well, and it is a shame to see people fail, not because their job performance is inadequate, but because they don't show basic courtesy. They become self-centered, arrogant, and downright rude!

Janice: In fact, basic courtesy is getting harder and harder to find in the business world, so those who do have it will stand out even more.

COURTESY COUNTS

Bill well remembers—though he wishes he could forget—the time he took a couple of top staffers on a business call to a prospect in Chicago. They were graciously ushered into the chairman's private dining room, where the chief sales VP on Bill's staff proceeded to spear the meat with his knife, dribble the juice on the tablecloth, and talk with his mouth full. What Bill remembers all too well was the chairman's stare, aimed directly at Bill as if to say, "You have a dog like this working in your organization, and you want my business?"

Although Bill fired the sales VP shortly thereafter, it took a long, long time before he got the chance to even go back and make his pitch to the Chicago prospect, much less gain his business.

> Politeness and consideration for others is like investing pennies and getting dollars back.
>
> —THOMAS SOWELL, COLUMNIST

Courtesy can make or break a career. We've seen it do both. We've seen people with everything going for them suddenly pull something like Bill's sales VP did—or wear an absolutely inappropriate dress to the client dinner—or scream at underlings for all to hear—or get in the elevator, where there's a captive audience, and talk about people and details that are not appropriate to the benign banter that qualifies as "elevator speak."

We've also seen people, often of only middling talent, rise high in the corporation because they always remembered to say please and thank you. Granted, that alone was not the cause of their rise, but when promotion time came around, they were the people who always came to mind, and their civility certainly helped smooth their upward climbs.

Manners are essential in any organization—whether the organization is a family of four or a corporation of four thousand. Manners separate us from animals; they're what allow civilization to flourish. Without common courtesy, life is a free-for-all. In business, that can be particularly dangerous. Imagine a business without discipline or structure; that's a business in serious trouble.

THE INTERVIEW

It starts with the interview—that all-important opportunity to make an impression. And where interview etiquette is concerned, Janice has seen it all.

There was the candidate who felt so comfortable in the interview—and granted, she had all the qualifications—that she came across as too informal. Her very relaxed manner said loud and clear that she took the company's acceptance of her for granted. That was simply off-key; after all, it was an interview for a professional position, not a chat between friends.

There was the candidate who was asked to wait in the conference room before the interview could begin. When the client went into the conference room to fetch him, he had his feet up on the conference table and was jabbering into his cell phone. Laid-back? Yes, and basically ill-mannered. Feet on the table is something you might do at home—your own home; it's certainly not something you do in a conference room when you are waiting to be interviewed and hoping to make an impression. This candidate made an impression, all right: he was out of the running before the interview began.

Everything counts in an interview. Why? There are probably a dozen people interviewing for this job—and five hundred more applicants to draw from if those twelve don't work out. Chances are that the twelve invited to be interviewed all have the basic requirements and are qualified for the position. So how will a recruiter like Janice distinguish among them? Simple. Whether consciously or not, she will judge the candidates on how they present themselves—not on their looks but on their grooming, their dress, how they comport themselves, their speech, how they sit, their eye contact, what jokes they laugh at, the questions they ask, whether they are affable, whether they are too affable. She'll also ask the receptionist how the candidate treated her, and she'll check with her assistant to see if the candidate left any sort of impression. When support staff tell recruiters like Janice that a candidate was rude or dismissive, it can be the absolute kiss of death.

In fact, Janice has put together a chart of interview tips as a guide for candidates, which we've reproduced on the next page. Yet what it all comes down to, as she says, is that "you have fourteen seconds to get across what's unique about you," and one fail-safe way of doing that is by demonstrating a high level of courtesy and a mastery of etiquette. Such a demonstration tells the interviewer that you know how to sincerely make a good impression—not just on a recruiter, but on employers, clients, and other employees. It's a signal that you have the poise to deal with others and the discipline to run a business operation. It makes you stand out—and that's the first step to being hired.

> **FAST FACT**
>
> It is estimated that 30 percent of all job interview failures are attributable to poor presentation skills and inadequate manners.

INTERVIEWING TIPS

1. Do arrive ahead of schedule for your interview.
2. Do develop the relationship: be friendly, but professional. Ask meaningful questions.
3. Do describe how you fit the specific position and how you can add value in the long term.
4. Do show interest in learning more, and do express career aspirations.
5. Do share relevant and non-confidential market information.
6. Do be candid, direct, honest, and professional.
7. Do let your genuine personality come through and make constant eye contact.
8. Do demonstrate your well-balanced approach to life by sharing your charitable activities, including not-for-profit boards.
9. In the way you carry yourself and interact, demonstrate the five Cs: Confidence, Credibility, Commitment, Courage, and Communication.
10. Do send a thank-you note after your meeting, concisely pointing out the highlights of how you fit with the organization, the position, and the potential boss.
11. Don't ask about other candidates being interviewed.
12. Don't divulge confidential information about other people or prior companies.
13. Don't bad-mouth others or former employers.
14. Don't interrupt the other person.
15. Don't laugh too loudly or inappropriately.
16. Don't dress inappropriately.
17. Don't be pompous, arrogant, and anxious about what the company can offer you.
18. Don't ask about compensation.
19. Don't drop names to impress others.
20. Don't appear anxious, yet do show interest.

Chadick Ellig ©, used by permission.

The reality is this: whether in an interview or on the job, in today's business world, where you're always onstage and are always being observed, your manners *will* define you—for good or for ill. Here's how to make sure your manners define you positively.

EXCELLENCE IN BUSINESS ETIQUETTE

First, let's define our terms. In our view, based on experience, business etiquette means treating other people in such a way that they feel special after an encounter with you—special enough that they *perform* better. If you can make every interaction with others at every level positive, you're not just striking a blow for courtesy, you're contributing to the improved performance of the organization. That marks you as good at your job at the very least—and as a leader at best.

In other words, business etiquette can be a business tool—a powerful business tool—and wielding it well can and will affect performance. So the first task in making sure you have business etiquette is to know what it's all about.

Task 1: Learn the Universal Standards of Etiquette

Basic etiquette is universal, and if you haven't learned it yet, now is the time. How should you study the subject? Are we suggesting you read Emily Post or Miss Manners? Absolutely. If you have failed to learn the basic lessons of courtesy, such fundamental primers are clearly necessary.

Or take a course; attend a seminar; watch how others do it. More and more businesses these days are offering etiquette courses to their employees for the precise reasons we've discussed: employees are woefully in arrears on the subject, and it is affecting business.

For example, *Forks for Dorks* is a wonderfully titled training unit on table manners. Essential for business? We refer you to the story that leads off this chapter—about Bill and his VP of sales—for the answer: yes! Table manners are absolutely essential. Meals are an obvious and frequent occasion for meetings, and learning how to conduct yourself at the table is an essential part of meeting strategy.

The chart that follows lists the key indicators of basic courtesy.

If you think you need to brush up on any of these—either because you're not sure how you stand or because there's a standard out there you've seen, admire, and aspire to—check it off. Then find a way to get the improving instruction you need.

Indicator	Feedback You Have Received	Needs Improvement?	Action Plan
Table Manners (Knows the Rules or Not)			
Dress (Fits the Company Style or Not)			
Appearance (Cleanliness, Hygiene, Neatness)			
Interview Manners (Asks Questions, Listens, Makes Eye Contact)			
Communication Style (Audible, Concise)			
Telephone (Responds to Calls, Pleasant in Greetings)			
E-mail (Replies Promptly)			
Listening (Asks Questions)			
Other			

Task 2: Learn the Particular Code of Your Organization—and of Your Boss

In addition to the universal standards of courtesy, there are codes, as mentioned earlier, within every organization that define such aspects of behavior as dress, meetings, presentations, use of the Internet, appearance, use of the telephone, and of course, your boss's own particular code. You need to learn these codes at the same time that you are mastering the universal standards of courtesy.

For example, what does "casual-dress Friday" actually mean in your organization? Does it mean one thing at the corporate level and something else in your department? Does it mean one thing for most Fridays but something else altogether if you're meeting the boss?

What's the story on Internet use in your organization? Can you do a little personal shopping on the Web? How about if you do it during lunch hour? What if you feel like shopping on "adult" sites? What's the code?

How are you supposed to answer the phone? If most people answer with a sullen "hello," won't you do yourself some good if you answer with your name and a pleasant "May I help you?"

You gained five pounds over the holidays, and you know you'll take them off at the gym, but in the meantime, does anyone care if your clothes fit a little tightly? Find out.

Again, here's a chart that will help you keep tabs on the rules of etiquette in your particular organization. Note the standard in the organization, and take special note of your boss's particular preferences vis-à-vis each etiquette indicator:

Indicator	Organizational Standard	Boss's Preference
Dress		
Appearance		

Indicator	Organizational Standard	Boss's Preference
Communication Style		
Telephone Conduct		
Internet Conduct		
E-mail Manners		
Other		

Add the two codes together—the particular codes of your organization and the universal codes of basic courtesy—and follow both. And if the two codes are at loggerheads, stick with basic courtesy; experience shows that if you practice standards of civility at all times, you can't lose.

APPEARANCES DON'T DECEIVE; THEY REVEAL

It is said that in social settings, appearance accounts for more than half of the first impression you make—55 percent, to be exact.

In business, 75 percent of the hiring decision may be based on appearance.

But isn't appearance deceptive? Isn't it just outward—on the surface? Not really. Outward appearance, after all, reflects the inner person and transmits a message about the effort you've made. That kind of "appearance" includes your dress, hygiene (clean nails, cleanly shaven, etc.), posture, neatness, speech, manner, and general comportment. And it tells a lot about you.

ETIQUETTE IN THE WORKPLACE

Universal standards of courtesy are particularly important in the workplace. Business relations are human relations—only more so. You're thrown together with people—not by choice—and must work with them to achieve a common goal. Your livelihood depends on achieving the goal, so getting along with the people is essential. Basic manners will do it, but particular attention to courtesy can turn the necessity of getting along into a tool of improved business performance.

> Good manners will open doors that the best education cannot.
>
> —CLARENCE THOMAS, JUSTICE OF THE U.S. SUPREME COURT

We see it every day: well-mannered executives are simply more likely to be effective leaders. They are sensitive to others; they listen better; they praise when they ask for something; and for those reasons, they can get the best out of people. In their hands, standards of courtesy become that powerful tool of business effectiveness we spoke of earlier. By the same token, when these standards are not applied, the workplace suffers, performance suffers, morale suffers, and invariably, the bottom line suffers.

TASK 3: IT'S A WORK ZONE; BE PARTICULARLY ATTENTIVE TO COURTESY

So now that you've learned the rules, it's essential to apply them. One way to do so is to think of courtesy as a business tool you can use tactically to advance strategic goals. Remember the old saying that you can "catch more flies with honey than with vinegar"? It applies in business as well. We'll mix our creature metaphors a bit and suggest that you perhaps think of yourself as a predatory shark in the cold, hostile waters of a cutthroat business. Won't you do better if you can lure other sharks to swim with you toward a common goal, and won't you be able to lure even more sharks with the office equivalent of honey—courtesy and attentiveness—rather than with harsh, vinegary behavior?

Moreover, there's a price to pay for not being courteous in the workplace. The same way that fines are doubled in highway work zones, ill-mannered behavior in the office can and will come back to haunt you. The reputation you forge today will not go away tomorrow; as we've said before, it's your skin—you can't go anywhere without it. A reputation as an individual no one wants to work with or for won't advance your career ambitions one iota. Instead, it can stall or reverse your hopes and dreams. By contrast, a reputation as someone fair, caring, and unfailingly courteous will get you past the work zone and tooling ahead at full speed on your career highway.

> Rudeness is the weak man's imitation of strength.
> —ERIC HOFFER, 1902–1983

But if all the codes and conventions and rules of etiquette and behavior you've been boning up on seem daunting, keep in mind that universal courtesy is based on simple decency and kindness. If you always do the kind and decent thing, you can't fail to be courteous—and when you're known for that kind of courtesy, using the wrong fork won't keep you from being promoted.

Here are some tips that are particularly important to apply in a work zone: First, there are the don'ts . . .

- Don't lose your cool. Ranting and raving are marks not of a powerful person, who wants what he wants when he wants it, but of someone who utterly lacks self-control.

- Don't use profanity. Yes, it may have its place in some work environments, and it can have its effect, but it needs to be used selectively and only in the right crowd. If in doubt, just forget about it.
- Don't get personal, don't get political, and leave religion out of it. That cuts two ways: Your coworkers don't need to know your personal history, political views, or religious faith or lack of it. And theirs should never be brought into the conversation either.
- Don't be late to meetings, presentations, or conferences. It's selfish—a statement that your time is more important than the time of those you are meeting.
- And once you get there, don't hog the floor. Even if you're the highest ranking or possibly even the most important person in the room—in fact, *especially* if you are—let others be heard.

Then there are the dos . . .

- Do practice small courtesies. We've said this before, but it is *so* worth repeating: you'll be stunned by the difference it makes if you always say, "Please," "Thank you," "You're welcome," and "Excuse me." Life will not only be more pleasant, but it will also be easier and will run more smoothly.
- Return phone calls; answer your e-mails—both promptly, no more than forty-eight hours later.
- The handwritten thank-you note after the interview, in praise of someone's performance, or to congratulate a colleague on a promotion or award is always appreciated —and could come back to reward you in the future.

In fact, all of these prohibitions and courtesies will be remembered—and they will define you in the eyes of both colleagues and those with power over your future. Just ask Janice. When she calls the people whom candidates have offered as references, she always asks how the referring person would describe the candidate. And she listens closely for comments about how the candidate deals with people. When people tell her that a particular candidate knows his or her etiquette, Janice makes special note of that; it indicates that the person interacts successfully with others, possesses integrity, and has a strong enough ego not to require that every project be a self-promotion. In short, if someone is described as "well mannered," the description distinguishes that person—and makes him or her a more likely and more attractive candidate.

SUMMARY

Etiquette can make or break a career. Failures of courtesy can mar a good performance record and keep an otherwise talented individual from rising in the organization. By contrast, following the codes of universal etiquette and of your organization's etiquette can serve as a powerful lubricant for an individual's upward path. Here are the basics:

1. Learn the universal standards of etiquette.
2. Learn the particular code of your organization—and of your boss.
3. Be particularly attentive to courtesy in the work zone.

Choose Your Car:
Learn How to Market Yourself

Janice: Does it seem to you that some people have green lights all along their career highway?

Bill: Certainly. Whatever the twists and turns, whatever the obstacles, they stay on track, hug the road, and end up in front. In fact, they probably run a few red lights.

Janice: I think the reason is that they market themselves well.

Bill: They market themselves as winners, and they are perceived as winners. Of course, there has to be something to market! You're a winner—how did you do it?

Janice: Thanks, but frankly, everyone has something they can market, some distinctive qualities they can claim for themselves. The trick is to position yourself so that you can show those qualities when the opportunity arises—and claim the prize. Bill, it's like your having run multiple businesses, published eighteen books, and still having time to give back, particularly to kids. You marketed you, but with a passion for everything you develop.

GAINING THE CAREER EDGE

We'll call them Tony and Jeff, like some championship NASCAR drivers we might name. Both ride in the very fastest lane and are on the same corporate track, where, for a while, there's room for both of them. Both are adept at swerving to avoid obstacles, staying off the soft shoulder, finding ways around the dead end, and gently maneuvering around that deer in the headlights. Tony tends to pull over more often than Jeff to offer roadside assistance, while Jeff just keeps blazing away.

But up ahead, the road narrows. The CFO slot is available, and while both men are obvious candidates, only one of them will win the job. Both are confident that they don't have to do a thing to get noticed. Assured of his stardom, Jeff keeps driving faster.

Tony slows down and thinks about it. He knows the CEO sees him; he's as visible as Jeff. But does the CEO know precisely what Tony can bring to the CFO job that will benefit the corporation? Maybe not. Maybe Tony had better let him know—and maybe he'd better recruit all those people he helped along the way to let the CEO know.

Tony swings into action. His supporters—all those people whose flat tires he helped fix—start a "support Tony" parade and are soon seen wearing lightweight twill jackets emblazoned with the slogan "Tony DRIVES!"

Jeff just keeps burning up the track, confident—justifiably—about his speed and performance.

When the checkered flag came down, it was Tony who had inched over the line first, and it was Jeff who found himself decidedly out of the race.

Bottom line? All things being equal, marketing—having a distinctive brand—is what makes the difference in a career. There's nothing false about branding yourself. It is smart.

Janice sees this branding as a key factor in the successful candidate. She hears it in her clients' responses to certain people: "I liked her unique style." "He was technically great, had the right experience, and was great interpersonally; he could make a difference at our company." "She will definitely fit in culturally." "He knows who he is, what he can bring to us." "She is a balanced person. Let's hire her." These star candidates, in Janice's experience, have a way of carving out their personalities or achievements or *something*, and communicating it in a way that draws people to them. The reason is simple: they're selling themselves—but doing it with style, honesty, and credibility.

BRAGGING RIGHTS

Don't confuse self-marketing with braggadocio, which the dictionary defines as "empty or pretentious bragging." What we are talking about is being aware of what you have to offer and demonstrating it to those who can benefit from it. It's as neat a formula as we know for advancing a career.

This is not a question of "getting noticed." You can dye your hair purple if all you want to do is get noticed. Rather, marketing yourself means positioning yourself for the right opportunity, so that when it turns up, you'll be ready to win it.

To whom should you market yourself? As we've said before, when it comes to support, you want a minimum of five people in the organization—preferably many more. Why five? So that even if one or two drop their support, you still have at least three individuals you know you can really count on and in whose eyes you are a winner.

To establish a brand identity, you have to know what people think of you. How do they describe you?

Task 1: Do the Market Research on Your Product—i.e., Yourself

You can't sell what you have to offer unless and until you know what that offering really consists of. And very often, people overlook what they have to offer as irrelevant. Nothing is irrelevant. Your accomplishments may run from making a direct hit on the corporation's bottom line to community involvement that directly impacted the company reputation. Your skills may include personal charm as well as financial wizardry. Your strengths may be evident from your last performance review, while your liabilities may actually be assets, if looked at in a different light. So Task 1 is to assess all of that: your skills, assets and liabilities, and accomplishments.

By skills, we mean the things you're good at—your competencies and talents, whether technical, social, intellectual, or experiential. Ten years of P&L experience counts as a skill, as does the ability to write well or to speak a foreign language.

"Assets and liabilities" means the special characteristics or essential traits that define you. Maybe you're very charming, charismatic—or not charming at all. Perhaps you're a good listener, or maybe you're a good talker. What is it about you that makes you a good driver on the career highway, and what may be holding you back?

Accomplishments are those achievements that you conceived and carried through to completion or those in which you participated from beginning to end. We don't mean something you *partly* worked on or a project that never got off the ground. What were the results to the company, and are the accomplishments still yielding those results?

In assessing your skills, assets and liabilities, and accomplishments, think of yourself as a product to be marketed, and divide your list into product features (what distinguishes you from others) and product benefits (how you make an impact). Here's a template:

BRAND IDENTITY

	My Product Features: Distinguishing Characteristics	My Product Benefits: Impact on the Organization
Skills		
Assets		
Liabilities		
Accomplishments		

Clarity is essential here—no fuzzy abstractions, please. Janice tells of how frustrating it is when candidates answer a question about what they're best at with clichés like, "I'm good at managing change," or "I like to build things." These say nothing.

"Oh, really?" Janice is apt to respond. "What have you built? Is it still standing today? If not, why not? Did the change you implemented work? How is it doing now?" Clarity above all.

TASK 2: LOOK IN THE REARVIEW MIRROR FOR ANOTHER TAKE ON THE PRODUCT—AND AIM FOR A TAGLINE

Back at Road Sign 9, you started a 360 survey to see how you were perceived by your peers. However far along you are in assessing how you're perceived by your peers and subordinates, add the results of that survey to the mix as market research on a product, the product being you.

You're aiming to find out how you're perceived on the career highway—whether you're seen as someone who guns the motor or eases into action, someone who brakes hard or starts fast but then slows down. Are you seen as taking shortcuts? Arriving on time or showing up late because you just felt like cruising?

Try to distill what you learn about yourself into five keywords—the five words everyone in your 360 poll would use about you.

1. _____

2. _____

3. _____

4. _____

5. _____

Sometimes, there's a gap between how you view yourself as a marketable product and how others view you. Analyze the gap now—use the three questions below—and create an action plan for closing the gap.

PERCEPTION GAPS

How I perceive/describe myself:
How others perceive/describe me:
What are the gaps—and how do I close them to create a positive marketing proposition for Brand Me?

TASK 3: DO A REALITY CHECK: HOW GOOD ARE YOUR DRIVING SKILLS?

Your research has yielded a fairly impressive set of products and features that you think you can market; and your 360 poll has given you a five-word tagline any advertiser would be proud to use. You're feeling like a veritable Boy Scout—trustworthy, loyal, friendly, cheerful, obedient, reverent, brave, and clean.

Now take those assessments and wash them through the final test of marketability. It's the tombstone-epitaph question—namely, what is your legacy? What will people say about you when you are gone? On the career highway, the only answer that matters is whether your accomplishments have been critical to the organization. So as you answer these next questions, do so within the context of your skills as a driver:

1. I am known for being a terrific person because:
2. I am known for my many accomplishments, which resulted in:
3. My bottom-line legacy on my career highway has been:
4. What I would really like someone to say about me while I am still alive:

TASK 4: PLAN A MARKETING CAMPAIGN FOR BRAND YOU

Once you've done a thorough reality check on your self-assessment and 360 assessment, you should have a clear picture of what you have to offer and how it can benefit the organization. That's your brand. It's what sets you apart in the organization; it's what you have to sell. Now it's time to make a plan and go sell it.

The experts tell us there are three essentials to any marketing campaign. It should excite people, make news, and include a call to action. That's precisely what you want to do for Brand *You*. From what you've learned in Tasks 1 through 3, find one thing about the product—i.e., you—that will excite a particular audience; in fact, find one thing for each audience you're trying to reach. Turn it into a newsworthy event—and ask your audience for something in return.

Donna D. had spent her high school years in Mexico, where her father was teaching at the university. She was fluent in Spanish, and her feeling for Hispanic culture was inherent. She realized this was a saleable commodity in an organization looking to expand its markets south of the U.S. border. But how to catch the attention of the Development Group that was working on the market expansion plan?

Donna's idea was to get herself invited to speak to the Latino Businessmen's Club in a nearby town. She wrote out a press release and made sure her appearance at the club was covered in the press. Then she sent the clippings, a copy of her speech, and a memo about the value she could bring to the Group to the head of Development. She was quickly brought into the Group and was assigned to liaise with Latino business organizations on both sides of the border. Her marketing campaign had been *muy bien*—a total success.

But what if you're one of those people who protests that you don't feel comfortable blowing your own horn? There's a simple, two-part answer to that. Part 1: If you don't blow your horn, who will? Part 2: If it doesn't get blown, who will hear it? Bottom line: stay silent and stay where you are; market yourself and move ahead. If you are not confident marketing your uniqueness, your personal features and benefits, and the positive impact on others, who will believe in you?

But no boasting, please. For one thing, contributing to the organization you work for is not something to boast about; it's your job. For another, in many organizations, the use of the word *I* is discouraged. Rightly so: in today's complex corporations, it's highly unlikely that any one, unassisted individual could single-handedly make a dramatic difference to the bottom line.

So do marketing, not boasting, and keep in mind that any marketing campaign needs to start with your understanding of the marketplace need. Then offer the unique selling proposition you can bring to answer that need (i.e., you), describe your product and its features and benefits in detail, focus on how the product differs from the competition, and offer a deal or present an "ask" that seeks a response from the "customer."

A good way to start is to follow an outline you might use in creating any sales brochure. We've reproduced it below, so you can write the brochure for Brand *You*:

BRAND *YOU*

1. The organizational need that you perceive:

   _____.

2. Your unique selling proposition—the distinctive value you can bring to answer the need:

   _____.

3. Product *You*: What are your features and benefits?

   _____.

4. Brand *You* bragging rights: what you've done that made a difference in contributing to the organization, and how it shows that you'll make a difference in the future:

   _____.

5. The "ask": what you're asking/offering, the deliverable response you seek:

   _____.

How do you execute the marketing plan? That is, how do you communicate the "brochure" for Brand *You*? Every which way you can. Everything you do in the organization, every task, every assignment, every favor given or asked is a marketing opportunity. The marketing experts have a great three-word phrase for it: "Build the brand,"—and take every chance you get to do so.

You have a presentation tomorrow? Make it an opportunity to both sell yourself *and* present the information you're showing—by letting people know the distinctive value you brought to the work. You have called in your direct reports for a confab? Let them know that your selling proposition is being there to help them—and that you're willing and eager to do so. You've been asked to make a speech at an industry conference? The speech is only the beginning. Make sure there's a press release, and make sure also that you print out a clean version of the speech and send it—along with any favorable press clippings and a nice note—to senior management.

Everywhere you can, in every meeting, with every memo, on every assignment, keep that horn blowing at a comfortable decibel level. You just want to be sure they hear the value of Brand *You*.

Task 5: Get Comfortable with Public Speaking. Now.

If all of this sounds like you're going to need to be comfortable speaking in public, you're right. There's no way around this necessity; you cannot communicate by being silent, and you cannot rely on others to communicate for you. But what do you do if you become tongue-tied at the very thought of being in the spotlight?

Practice.

Know what it is you want to say and rehearse it. Rehearse it in front of the mirror, rehearse it in the shower, rehearse it before your spouse and children. Then rehearse it some more.

If you start off nervous, don't worry. If you feel your knees shaking and your voice wavering, *that's natural.* Press on, and your legs will stop bobbing and your voice will get stronger.

Tell yourself you are simply telling somebody something it's important for that person to know. If it's a big audience, spot a single person in the audience to be that somebody . . . then spot another person . . . then another . . . another.

Say what you have to say simply. Above all, say it with energy.

And when you have finished saying what you came to say, stop talking. You're done.

SUMMARY

Even if you handle all the road signs on your career highway with professionalism and good sense, the extra edge in a career comes from marketing yourself successfully. Here's how to do it:

1. Do the market research on your product—i.e., yourself.
2. Look in the rearview and side mirrors for another take on the product—and aim for a tagline.
3. How good are your driving skills? Do a reality check of the critical accomplishments you can truly claim for yourself.
4. Plan a marketing campaign for Brand *You*.
5. Get comfortable with public speaking. *Now*.

Your Career Highway

Janice: Well, Bill, are we at the end of the road?

Bill: The beginning.

Janice: And where are our readers headed?

Bill: To a bright future—if they've done the work of this book.

Janice: Absolutely. If they've done the work of this book, they're on their way to a successful future—and they'll be driving there in the fast lane.

Bill: And passing just about all the other cars on the career highway.

EQUIPPED AND READY

An awful lot of cars these days are equipped with global positioning systems. It means their drivers always know exactly where they are, have a record of exactly where they've been, and can see exactly where they're going. If you've done the work of this book, you've equipped your career car with its own GPS—a system sufficient to have you tooling along in the passing lane at top speed.

The work you've done in these past nineteen chapters hasn't been easy. We warned you about that way back in the Introduction—remember? But if you've done it conscientiously, carefully, with thought and reflection, you've learned a lot, analyzed a lot, and achieved a lot.

Think about it:

- You've stopped to reevaluate your career and your life, looking closely in your rearview mirror and making sure you can see the road ahead clearly.
- You may have taken yourself in hand to change directions entirely, exiting one career highway to look for and embark on another. If so, it was no easy task, although it was essential if you were going to live your dream.
- You've very possibly strategized your way out of a dead-end career and driven in reverse out of a blind alley into the sunlight. A tough call—tough to pull off.
- You've worked to mobilize the power within you so you stop being a victim.
- You've also learned how to adapt to a changing organization, industry, economy, culture, or job situation.
- You've figured out how to reinvent yourself and keep on reinventing yourself, how to steer your way through some slippery corporate politics, how to manage your boss—and your peers—and how to compete to win.
- You know what to do about romance on the job, about caring for a family at home, about how to integrate life and work and be a truly good citizen of your community and the world.
- You're prepared to read an organization's unwritten rules, deal with doors that are closed in your face, stay off the

soft shoulder of dubious ethical behavior, even go to dinner with a prospective client and not use the wrong fork.
- You're ready to market yourself for who you are—and for the unique talent you offer.

In fact, you might find it helpful to continue to review the actions you take on your career highway, and we've created a template that will help you with your review. It asks you to clarify and summarize what you've done and what you've learned at three-month, six-month, and twelve-month milestones.

PROGRESS REPORT: HOW AM I DOING?

Actions I've Taken
3-Month Review of Actions Taken
6-Month Review of Actions Taken
12-Month Review of Actions Taken

There's a good reason for all this work of review and distillation. The reason is this: your career is worth it.

From his solitary cabin on Walden Pond, Henry David Thoreau wrote long ago that he knew of "no more encouraging fact than the unquestionable ability of man to elevate his life by a conscious endeavor." Your career is a conscious endeavor that can elevate your life to great heights of fulfillment and can yield rewards that go well beyond the material. It can fulfill your expectations and your ambitions—and it can help you define both. Certainly, those are encouraging facts.

The dictionary defines a career as "a chosen pursuit" and as "the general course or progression of one's working life." It's both; in the terms we've used throughout this book, it's simultaneously the highway you choose to drive and the way you drive it. You will spend at least a third of your life on this highway, and the ride can be pleasant, exhilarating, comfortable, and uplifting.

It's all up to you.

You're in the driver's seat. Your hands are on the steering wheel. Your foot is on the gas pedal. You're in control. You determine the air temperature, who's riding with you, even what's playing on the radio.

Ease out of this parking space. Make your turn. Find your lane. Get ready to elevate your life.

You are in charge. Take the wheel. Accelerate. You are CEO of your career.

ABOUT THE AUTHORS

JANICE REALS ELLIG

Janice Reals Ellig is the Co-CEO of Chadick Ellig, a New York City-based executive search firm. With more than twenty years as a corporate executive, she has worked extensively on leadership issues with top management and boards of directors.

Previously, Janice was a senior vice president at Ambac Financial Group, a diversified financial services company, where she was responsible for corporate marketing, human resources, and administration. A member of Ambac's Executive Committee, she helped take the company public after a spin-off from Citibank in 1991.

Prior to Ambac, Janice held positions at Citigroup, where she had worldwide human resources responsibility for the Global Insurance Division and at Pfizer in the Consumer Products Division.

She holds a master's degree in Organizational Development from Rider College and a bachelor of Business Administration degree from the University of Iowa. She is currently a board director of the University of Iowa Foundation, a Vice Chair of the NYC YMCA Board of Greater New York City, and a member of the Business Committee of the Metropolitan Museum of Art in New York. Janice also serves as a member of the Women's Forum and The Economic Club of New York.

Janice has been quoted in the *Wall Street Journal, USA Today*, the *New York Times*, the *Chicago Tribune, Fortune* magazine, and other publications. She has appeared on *Power Lunch*, Bloomberg, and CNN, as well as radio, and on-line to talk about career management in general and women's issues in particular. In 2002, Janice received the award for excellence in promoting the "Economic Development of Women" at the Gala Celebrating Women Who Make a Difference, under the auspices of WLIW 21, Long Island's public broadcasting station. In 2001, Janice co-authored, with Bill Morin,

What Every Successful Woman Knows—12 Breakthrough Strategies to Get the Power and Ignite Your Career (McGraw Hill, 2001).

WILLIAM J. MORIN

Bill Morin is the founder and chairman of WJM Associates, Inc. He established the venture in 1996, following a twenty-two-year career as chairman and chief executive officer of Drake Beam Morin, Inc., the international career continuation and organizational consulting firm. At DBM, Bill worked closely with senior managers at more than two hundred Fortune 500 corporations on a range of human resources management issues.

Holder of a master's degree from Southern Illinois University, Bill began his career at General Foods Corporation as an operations supervisor and later held manufacturing, marketing, sales, and human resources positions at Avon Products and Cole National Corporation.

Bill has coached countless senior-level Fortune 500 executives and has authored and coauthored books and articles about trust in the organization, job search techniques, coping with job loss, and corporate revitalization. He has been a frequent guest on network television and is quoted often in the business press. His network appearances have included *Good Morning America, Today*, CNN's *Pinnacle*, the *ABC Nightly News*, and Jim Lehrer's *NewsHour*. He regularly covers career management on CNBC and was host of the highly acclaimed two-hour, live television program on careers sponsored by the U.S. Chamber of Commerce—*Modern Career Management*. He is also the regular career guidance advisor on the "Employment Channel" viewed in New York's metro area.

Bill serves as a board member for the United Earth Foundation and is an Ellis Island Award winner. He was named "Corporate Leader of the Year" in 1995 by the National Women's Economic Alliance Foundation.

ACKNOWLEDGMENTS

We are pleased to acknowledge the wonderful support and advice from family, friends, and collaborators that went into the writing of this book.

Both of us are grateful to Bruce Ellig, former Global Head of Human Resources for Pfizer, whose experience and expertise were invaluable in helping us identify the relevant road signs so we could help readers navigate through, past, or around them as CEOs in charge of their careers.

To our editor, Susanna Margolis, who worked with us on our first book together, *What Every Successful Woman Knows: 12 Breakthrough Strategies to Get the Power and Ignite Your Career,* thanks for clarifying the road signs as true markers that help readers take the wheel. You've helped make this an insightful and rewarding ride.

We want to thank the people at Thomas Nelson for their expertise, professionalism, and good will in making this book happen: Senior Editor Kristen Parrish for her astute editing and constant encouragement, Marketing Director Dave Schroeder for his enthusiasm, creativity and insightful planning, and Victor Oliver for seeing the book's message as an essential one for professionals seeking to build on or change their careers-and for leading the way to making this book a reality. Barbara Cave Henricks, your creative public relations/marketing solutions demonstrated the uniqueness of our book and value to readers in their ever changing work environments. And to our agent, Al Longden of Rights Unlimited, who worked with great calm and encouragement, we offer our gratitude.

A significant advisor and confidante in Janice's life was her sister, Adrienne. As a successful career woman in hospital administration, Adrienne's legacy is an abiding spirit and a shining inspiration that lives on through the masters-level women who are the recipients of a scholarship in her name.

Janice would like to thank Chris Gratz and Jeannie Masterson, for their assistance in editing the manuscript and all Chadick Ellig search professionals who truly are outstanding—Deborah Blumenthal, Tamara Brennan, Jason Brown, Pat Erdman, Cathy Fleming, Janice Joseph, Lan Nguyen, Natasha Novokhatskaya, Nim Ratanakul, Anne Szeto, and Managing Director Stacy Lauren Musi. To her partner, Susan Chadick, with whom she shares the exhilarating ride of "*Executive Search*" daily, Janice offers a sincere thank-you for being a supportive business colleague and friend.

Bill gratefully acknowledges the positive impact of his loving sister, Martha, on his early and professional life. During the writing of this book, Martha succumbed to a lengthy battle with breast cancer, but she met the challenges that go with such a battle valiantly and with determination.

Bill's thanks also go to the great team at WJM Associates, who daily make superb efforts to improve their performance and that of others. Cynthia Auman-King, Rick Cumberland, Marilyn Kaufman, Dale Klamfoth, Scott Litchfield, Jennie Migliore, Tim Morin, Chrystal Sanchez, Francie Sinnott, Randall Thames, and Kip Trum: they constitute a team of professionals like no other.

Bill and Janice extend their appreciation to the many clients and candidates with whom they have had the privilege to work. Thanks to all our clients for taking us into your confidence, for the business you entrusted us with, and for the friendship we have enjoyed with you. Our experiences with you have helped to make *Driving the Career Highway* possible.

We hope our book helps all readers be the CEO in Charge of their Careers as they head toward their destination. May the ride along your career highway be the ride of a lifetime—and a ride that you control.

NOTES

Road Sign 9: Falling Rocks
1. Ken Blanchard and Sheldon Bowles, *Raving Fans: A Revolutionary Approach to Customer Service* (William Morrow, 1993).

Road Sign 10: Road Narrows
1. Excerpted from *The American Heritage Dictionary of the English Language,* Third Edition Copyright © 1992 by Houghton Mifflin Company. Electronic version licensed from Lernout & Hauspie Speech Products N.V., further reproduction and distribution restricted in accordance with the Copyright Law of the United States. All rights reserved.

Road Sign 11: Danger Zone
1. Janice Reals Ellig and William J. Morin, *What Every Successful Woman Knows: 12 Breakthrough Strategies to Get the Power and Ignite Your Career* (McGraw Hill, 2001).

Road Sign 12: Watch Children
1. Fact sheet: National Trends for Women-Owned Businesses, www.womensbusinessresearch.org/freepublications/ USFiftyPercentorMore-Owned.pdf.
2. www.simmons.edu/about/news/releases/2002/10_22_02_teen_ business.shtml.

Road Sign 13: Emergency Stopping Only
1. www.heldrich.rutgers.edu/Resources/Publication/65/ release399.399.doc.

Road Sign 14: Adopt a Highway
1. AAFRC Foundation press release, www.aafrc.org/press_releases/ trustreleases/charityholds.html.

Road Sign 16: Do Not Enter
1. 2005 Catalyst Census of Women Board of Directors of the Fortune 500, www.catalystwpmen.org/pressroom/press_ releases/3_29_06%20WBD%20release.pdf.

Road Sign 17: Soft Shoulder
1. American Management Association 2002 Survey of Corporate Values. www.amanet.org/researchy/pdfs/2002_corp_value.pdf.